SCHAUM
EASY OUTLINES

College Chemistry

Second Edition

**Jerome L. Rosenberg
and Lawrence M. Epstein**

**Abridgement Editor:
Philip H. Rieger**

New York   Chicago   San Francisco   Lisbon   London   Madrid   Mexico City
Milan   New Delhi   San Juan   Seoul   Singapore   Sydney   Toronto

The McGraw·Hill Companies

1 2 3 4 5 6 7 8 9 10 11 12 13 14 15   WFR/WFR   1 9 8 7 6 5 4 3 2 1 0

ISBN   978-0-07-174587-1
MHID   0-07-174587-4

Library of Congress Cataloging-in-Publication Data

Rosenberg, Jerome Laib, 1921-
      Schaum's easy outline of college chemistry / Jerome Rosenberg. — 2nd ed.
           p.   cm. — (Schaum's outlines)
      Includes index.
      ISBN 0-07-174587-4 (alk. paper)
        1. Chemistry—Outlines, syllabi, etc.   2. Chemistry—Problems, exercises,
      etc.   I. Title   II. Title: Easy outline of college chemistry.

      QD41.G668   2010
      540—dc22   2010010890

McGraw-Hill books are available at special quantity discounts to use as premiums and sales promotions or for use in corporate training programs. To contact a representative, please e-mail us at bulksales@mcgraw-hill.com.

This book is printed on acid-free paper.

Contents

Online Diagnostic Test

Go to **Schaums.com** to launch the Schaum's Diagnostic Test.

This convenient application provides a 30-question multiple-choice test that will pinpoint areas of strength and weakness to help you focus your study. Questions cover all aspects of college chemistry, and the correct answers are explained in full. With a question-bank that rotates daily, the Schaum's Online Test also allows you to check your progress and readiness for final exams.

Other titles featured in Schaum's Online Diagnostic Test:

Schaum's Easy Outlines: Geometry, 2nd Edition
Schaum's Easy Outlines: Calculus, 2nd Edition
Schaum's Easy Outlines: Statistics, 2nd Edition
Schaum's Easy Outlines: Elementary Algebra, 2nd Edition
Schaum's Easy Outlines: College Algebra, 2nd Edition
Schaum's Easy Outlines: Biology, 2nd Edition
Schaum's Easy Outlines: Human Anatomy and Physiology, 2nd Edition
Schaum's Easy Outlines: Organic Chemistry, 2nd Edition
Schaum's Easy Outlines: Beginning Chemistry, 2nd Edition

Chapter 1
QUANTITIES AND UNITS

Introduction

Most of the measurements and calculations in chemistry are concerned with quantities such as pressure, volume, mass, and energy. Every quantity includes both a number and a unit. The *unit* simultaneously identifies the kind of dimension and the magnitude of the reference quantity used as a basis for comparison. The *number* indicates how many of the reference units are contained in the quantity being measured. If we say that the mass of a sample is 20 grams, we mean that the mass is 20 times the mass of 1 gram, the unit of mass chosen for comparison. Although *20 grams* has the dimension of mass, *20* is a pure dimensionless number, being the ratio of two masses, that of the sample and that of the reference, 1 gram.

Significant Figures

The numerical value of every observed measurement is an approximation, since no physical measurement—of temperature, mass, volume, etc.—is ever exact. The accuracy of a measurement is always limited by the reliability of the measuring instrument.

Suppose that the recorded length of an object is 15.7 cm. By convention, this means that the length was measured to the *nearest* 0.1 cm and that its exact value lies between 15.65 and 15.75 cm. If this measurement were exact to the nearest 0.01 cm, it would have been recorded as 15.70 cm. We say that the first measurement is accurate to 3 significant figures and the second to 4.

A recorded volume of 2.8 L represents two significant figures. If this same volume were written 0.028 m^3, it would still contain only two significant figures. Zeroes appearing as the first digits of a number are not significant, since they merely locate the decimal point.

We often use *scientific notation* to express very large or very small numbers, indicating the number of significant figures by the number multiplied by 10^x. Thus, for example,

$$22400 = 2.24 \times 10^4 \qquad 0.00306 = 3.06 \times 10^{-3}$$

When two exponentials are multiplied (or divided), the exponents are added (or subtracted). For example,

$$(1.5 \times 10^5) \times (2.0 \times 10^{-3}) = 3.0 \times 10^2$$

$$(4.0 \times 10^7)/(2.0 \times 10^2) = 2.0 \times 10^5$$

When an exponential is raised to a power, the exponents are multiplied; for example,

$$(10^4)^{-2} = 10^{-8} \qquad (10^6)^{1/2} = 10^3$$

Some numbers are exact. These include π (3.14159...), numbers arising from counting (e.g., the number of experimental determinations of an observed measurement), and numbers which involve a definition (the mass of one atom of ^{12}C is exactly 12 u and the conversion of cm to m involves exactly 10^{-2} m/cm).

A number is rounded off to the desired number of significant figures by dropping one or more digits from the right. When the first digit dropped is less than 5, the last digit retained should remain unchanged; when it is greater than 5, the last digit is rounded up. When the digit dropped is exactly 5, the number retained is rounded up or down to get an even number. When more than one digit is dropped, rounding off should be done in a block, not one digit at a time.

Illustration:

The following numbers are accurate to two significant figures: 2.3, 0.023, 2.3×10^4.

The following numbers are rounded to two significant figures: $64500 \to 6.4 \times 10^4$, $5.75 \to 5.8$, $1.653 \to 1.7$, $1.527 \to 1.5$

Propagation of Errors

When we perform a calculation using numbers of limited accuracy, the result should be written with the appropriate number of significant figures.

When we add or subtract numbers, the number of significant figures in the answer is limited by the number with the smallest number of significant figures to the right of the decimal, e.g.,

$$4.20 + 1.6523 + 0.015 = 5.8673 \to 5.87$$

This rule is an approximation to a more exact statement that the error in a sum or difference is the square root of the sum of the squares of the errors in the numbers being added or subtracted. Thus in the above example, the error in the result is

$$\sqrt{(0.01)^2 + (0.0001)^2 + (0.001)^2} = 0.010$$

When multiplying or dividing two numbers, the result should contain only as many significant figures as the least accurate factor without regard for the position of the decimal point, e.g.,

$$7.485 \times 8.61 = 64.4 \qquad\qquad 0.1642/1.52 = 0.108$$

This rule is an approximation to a more exact statement that the fractional error of a product or quotient is the square root of the sum of the squares of the fractional errors in the numbers being multiplied or divided.

Thus in the above examples, the fractional and absolute errors in the results are:

$$\sqrt{\left(\frac{0.001}{7.485}\right)^2 + \left(\frac{0.01}{8.61}\right)^2} = 0.0012 \qquad 0.0012 \times 64.4 = 0.08 \approx 0.1$$

$$\sqrt{\left(\frac{0.0001}{0.1642}\right)^2 + \left(\frac{0.01}{1.52}\right)^2} = 0.0066 \qquad 0.0066 \times 0.108 = 0.0007 \approx 0.001$$

The approximate and more exact approaches sometimes lead to different results when numbers beginning with 1 or 2 are involved. For example, 9.84/8.9 = 1.106. The approximate method suggests writing the result to two significant figures, 1.1, but the more exact method leads to relative error of 0.011 and an absolute error of 0.012, so that writing the result with three significant figures, 1.11, is appropriate.

When propagating errors through more complex expressions, two or more steps of error estimation may be needed. For example,

$$29.7 \times (7.250 + 3.6554) = 29.7 \times 10.905 = 324$$

Remember:

Approximate rules for propagation of errors:

- When adding or subtracting numbers, the number of significant figures to the right of the decimal determines the accuracy of the result.

- When multiplying or dividing numbers, the total number of significant figures determines the accuracy of the result.

The International System of Units

Dimensional calculations are greatly simplified if a consistent set of units is employed. The three major reference dimensions for mechanics are *length, mass,* and *time*, but length can be measured in units of inches, feet, centimeters, meters, etc. Which should be used? The scientific community has made considerable progress toward a common system of reference units. This system is known as SI from the French name *Systéme International d'Unités*. In SI, the reference units for *length, mass,* and *time* are the *meter, kilogram,* and *second*, with symbols m, kg, and s, respectively.

To express quantities much larger or smaller than the standard units, multiples or submultiples of these units are used, as shown in the Table 1-1. Thus, 10^{-12} s is a picosecond (ps), and 10^3 m is a kilometer (km). Since for historical reasons the SI reference unit for mass, the kilogram, already has a prefix, multiples for mass should be derived by applying the multiplier to the unit *gram* rather than to the *kilogram*. Thus 10^{-9} kg is a microgram (10^{-6} g), abbreviated μg.

Table 1-1 Multiples and Submultiples for Units

Prefix	Abbr.	Multiplier	Prefix	Abbr.	Multiplier
deci	d	10^{-1}	deka	da	10
centi	c	10^{-2}	hecto	h	10^2
milli	m	10^{-3}	kilo	k	10^3
micro	μ	10^{-6}	mega	M	10^6
nano	n	10^{-9}	giga	G	10^9
pico	p	10^{-12}	tera	T	10^{12}

Many non-SI units remain in common use; some of these are given in the Table 1-2.

Compound units can be derived by applying algebraic operations to the simple units. For example, the SI units of volume and density are m^3 and kg/m^3, since

$$\text{Volume} = \text{length} \times \text{length} \times \text{length} = m \times m \times m = m^3$$

$$\text{density} = \frac{\text{mass}}{\text{volume}} = \frac{kg}{m^3}$$

Table 1-2 Some SI and Common Non-SI Units

Quantity	Unit Name	Unit Symbol	Definition
length	angstrom	Å	10^{-10} m
	inch	in	2.54×10^{-2} m
volume	cubic meter	m^3	(SI unit)
	liter	L	10^{-3} m^3
	cubic centimeter	cm^3, mL	10^{-6} m^3
mass	atomic mass unit	u	1.6605×10^{-27} kg
	pound	lb	0.45359 kg
density	gram per milliliter	g/mL or g/cm^3	10^3 kg/m^3
force	newton	N	kg·m/s² (SI unit)

Note that symbols for multiplied units may be separated by a dot or a space, e.g., kg•s or kg s. Symbols for divided units may be written with a solidus or an exponent, e.g., m/s or m•s^{-1} or m s^{-1}.

Temperature is an independent dimension which cannot be defined in terms of mass, length, and time. The SI unit of temperature is the *kelvin* (K), defined as 1/273.16 times the *triple point* temperature of water (the temperature at which ice, liquid water, and water vapor coexist at equilibrium). 0 K is the absolute zero of temperature.

On the *Celsius* (or *centigrade*) scale, a temperature difference of 1°C is 1 K (exactly). The normal boiling point of water is 100°C, the normal freezing point 0°C, and absolute zero –273.15°C. On the *Fahrenheit* scale, a temperature difference of 1°F is 5/9 K (exactly). The boiling point and freezing point of water, and absolute zero are 212°F, 32°F and –459.67°F, respectively. Conversions from one temperature scale to another make use of the following equations:

$$t/°C = T/K - 273.15$$

$$t/°F = (9/5)(t/°C) + 32$$

In these equations, we have used a particularly convenient notation: $t/°C$, T/K, and $t/°F$ refer to the numerical values of temperatures on the Celsius, Kelvin, and Fahrenheit scales. By dividing the temperature in degrees Celsius by 1°C, we obtain a pure number.

There Is Good News and Bad News!

The good news is that the SI system of units is consistent so that substitution of quantities with SI units into an equation will give a result in SI units.

The bad news is that many chemical calculations involve non-SI units.

Dimensional Analysis

Units are a necessary part of the specification of a physical quantity. When physical quantities are subjected to mathematical operations, the units must be carried along with the numbers and must undergo the same operations as the numbers. Quantities cannot be added or subtracted directly unless they have not only the same dimensions but also the same units, for example:

$$6 \text{ L} + 2 \text{ L} = 8 \text{ L} \qquad (5 \text{ cm})(2 \text{ cm}^2) = 10 \text{ cm}^3$$

In solving problems, one often can be guided by the units to the proper way of combining the given values. Some textbooks refer to this method as the *factor-label* or *unit-factor* method; we will call it *dimensional analysis*. In essence, one goes from a given unit to the desired unit by multiplying or dividing such that unwanted units cancel. For example, consider converting 5.00 inches to centimeters, given the conversion factor 2.54 cm/in. We might try two approaches:

$$5.00 \text{ in} \times \frac{\text{in}}{2.54 \text{ cm}} = 1.97 \text{ in}^2/\text{cm} \qquad 5.00 \text{ in} \times \frac{2.54 \text{ cm}}{\text{in}} = 12.7 \text{ cm}$$

The first try gives nonsensical units, signaling a misuse of the conversion factor. On the second try, the inch units cancel, leaving the desired centimeter units.

Estimation of Numerical Answers

If you input the numbers correctly into your calculator, the answer will be correct. But will you recognize an incorrect answer? You will if you obtain an approximate answer by visual inspection. Especially important is the order of magnitude, represented by the location of the decimal point or the power of 10, which may go astray even though the digits are correct. For example, consider a calculation of the power required to raise a 639 kg mass 20.74 m in 2.120 minutes:

$$\frac{639 \text{ kg} \times 20.74 \text{ m} \times 9.81 \text{ m s}^{\pm 2}}{2.120 \text{ min} \times 60 \text{ s/min}} = 1022 \text{ J/s} = 1022 \text{ watts}$$

This example involves concepts and units which may be unfamiliar to you, so that you can't easily judge whether the result "makes sense," so we'll check the answer by estimation. Write each term in exponential notation, using just one significant figure. Then mentally combine the powers of 10 and the multipliers separately to estimate the result:

$$\frac{6 \times 10^2 \times 2 \times 10^1 \times 1 \times 10^1}{2 \times 6 \times 10^1} = \frac{12 \times 10^4}{12 \times 10^1} = 1000$$

The estimate agrees with the calculation to one significant figure, showing that the calculation is very likely correct.

Problems

1.1 The color of light depends on its wavelength. Red light has a wavelength on the order of 7.8×10^{-7} m. Express this length in micrometers, in nanometers, and in angstroms.
Ans. 0.78 μm, 780 nm, 7800 Å

1.2 The blue iridescence of butterfly wings is due to striations that are 0.15 μm apart, as measured by an electron microscope. What is this distance in centimeters? How does this spacing compare with the wavelength of blue light, about 4500 Å?
Ans. 1.5×10^{-5} cm, 1/3 the wavelength

1.3 In a crystal of Pt, individual atoms are 2.8 Å apart along the direction of closest packing. How many atoms would lie on a 1.00-cm length of a line in this direction? *Ans.* 3.5×10^7

1.4 The bromine content of average ocean water is 65 parts by weight per million. Assuming 100% recovery, how many cubic meters of ocean water must be processed to produce 0.61 kg of bromine? Assume that the density of sea water is 1.0×10^3 kg/m^3.

Ans. 9.4 m^3

1.5 Find the volume in liters of 40 kg of carbon tetrachloride, whose density is 1.60 g/cm^3. *Ans.* 25 L

1.6 A sample of concentrated sulfuric acid is 95.7% H_2SO_4 by weight and its density is 1.84 g/cm^3. (a) How many grams of pure H_2SO_4 are contained in one liter of the acid? (b) How many cubic centimeters of acid contain 100 g of pure H_2SO_4?

Ans. (a) 1.76×10^3 g; (b) 56.8 cm^3

1.7 A quick method of determining density utilizes Archimedes' principle, which states that the buoyant force on an immersed object is equal to the weight of the liquid displaced. A bar of magnesium metal attached to a balance by a fine thread weighed 31.13 g in air and 19.35 g when completely immersed in hexane (density 0.659 g/cm^3). Calculate the density of this sample of magnesium in SI units. *Ans.* 1741 kg/m^3

1.8 A piece of gold leaf (density 19.3 g/cm^3) weighing 1.93 mg can be beaten into a transparent film covering an area of 14.5 cm^3. What is the volume of 1.93 mg of gold? What is the thickness of the transparent film in angstroms?

Ans. 1.00×10^{-4} cm^3, 690 Å

1.9 Sodium metal has a very wide liquid range, melting at 98°C and boiling at 892°C. Express the liquid range in degrees Celsius, kelvins, and degrees Fahrenheit. *Ans.* 794°C, 794 K, 1429°F

Chapter 2
MOLES AND EMPIRICAL FORMULAS

IN THIS CHAPTER:

✔ *Atoms and Isotopes*
✔ *Relative Atomic Masses*
✔ *Moles and Molar Masses*
✔ *Empirical Formula from Composition*
✔ *Chemical Formulas from Mass Spectrometry*

Atoms and Isotopes

In the atomic theory proposed by John Dalton in 1805, all atoms of a given element were assumed to be identical. Eventually it was realized that atoms of a given element are not necessarily identical; an element can exist in several *isotopic* forms that differ in atomic mass.

Every atom has a positively charged nucleus and one or more electrons that form a charge cloud surrounding the nucleus. The nucleus contains over 99.9% of the total mass of the atom. Every nucleus may be described as being made up of two different kinds of particles, *protons* and *neutrons*, collectively called *nucleons*. Protons and neutrons have nearly the same mass, but only the proton is charged, so that the total charge of a nucleus is equal to the number of protons times the charge of one proton. The magnitude of the proton charge is equal to that of the electron so that a neutral atom has an equal number of protons and electrons.

The atoms of all isotopes of an element have the same number of protons, the *atomic number*, Z. The nuclei of different isotopes differ, however, in the number of neutrons and therefore in the total number of nucleons per nucleus. The total number of nucleons is A, the *mass number*. Atoms of different isotopic forms of an element, *nuclides*, are distinguished by using the mass number as a left superscript on the symbol of the element, e.g., ^{15}N refers to the isotope of N with mass number 15.

You Need to Know

Atomic nuclei contain protons and neutrons.

- An element is defined by the nuclear charge; the atomic number Z = number of protons.

- Mass number A = no. protons + no. neutrons.

- Isotopes of an element have the same Z, but different A's.

Relative Atomic Masses

Because the mass of an atom is very small, it is convenient to define a special unit that avoids large negative exponents. This unit, called the *atomic mass unit* and designated by the symbol u (some authors use the abbreviation amu), is defined as exactly 1/12 the mass of a ^{12}C atom.

Thus the mass of a ^{12}C atom is exactly 12 u. The masses and abundances of some other nuclides are listed in Table 2-1.

Naturally occurring silicon is 92.23% ^{28}Si, 4.67% ^{29}Si, and 3.10% ^{30}Si. For chemical purposes, it is sufficient to know the *average mass* of a silicon atom in this isotopic mixture. These average masses are designated by $A_r(E)$, where E is the symbol for the particular element. For example, the average mass of silicon atoms is

$$A_r(Si) = 0.9223 \times 27.977 + 0.0467 \times 28.976 + 0.0310 \times 29.974 = 28.085$$

The term *atomic mass* will be understood to mean average atomic mass; *nuclidic mass* refers to one particular isotope of an element. Atomic masses are used in nearly all chemical calculations.

Table 2-1. Some Nuclidic Masses in Atomic Mass Units

^{1}H	99.985%	1.00783 u	^{16}O	99.76 %	15.99491 u
^{2}H	0.015	2.01410	^{17}O	0.04	16.99913
^{12}C	98.89	12.00000	^{18}O	0.20	17.99916
^{13}C	1.11	13.00335	^{28}Si	92.23	27.97693
^{14}N	99.64	14.00307	^{29}Si	4.67	28.97649
^{15}N	0.36	15.00011	^{30}Si	3.10	29.97377
^{32}S	95.0	31.97207	^{34}S	4.22	33.96786

Remember:

Nuclidic mass = mass of a particular nuclide, relative to mass of ^{12}C, exactly 12 u. Atomic masses, A_r, commonly found in tables, are averages of nuclidic masses, weighted to reflect the isotopic composition of the elements.

Moles and Molar Masses

Most chemical experiments involve enormous numbers of atoms or molecules. For this reason, the SI system of units defines the *mole*, abbreviated mol, as the amount of a substance that contains the same number of atoms as 12 g of ^{12}C. This number is called *Avogadro's number*, $N_A = 6.0221 \times 10^{23}$ mol^{-1}. The mole thus is a counting term analogous to "dozen." Just as a dozen eggs corresponds to 12 eggs, a mole of atoms is 6.0221×10^{23} atoms. The mole can be applied to counting atoms, molecules, ions, electrons, protons, neutrons, etc.—it always corresponds to N_A of the counted species. The mass of one mole of an element with atomic mass $A_r(E)$ u is $N_A A_r$ u or simply A_r g/mol, e.g., the atomic mass of gold is 197.0 u, and the mass of one mole of gold atoms is 197.0g.

One mole of atoms, molecules, ions, etc., contains one Avogadro's number ($N_A = 6.0221 \times 10^{23}$ mol^{-1}) of that species.

The chemical symbol for an element—H, C, O, etc.—is used to designate that element. Molecular substances consist of independent molecules containing two or more atoms bound together. A molecular formula specifies the identity and number of the atoms in the molecule. For instance, the formula for carbon dioxide is CO_2, one carbon atom and two oxygen atoms. The molecular mass of CO_2 is $A_r(C) + 2A_r(O) = 12.0107 + 2 \times 15.9994 = 44.0095$ u. The *molar mass* of CO_2 is the mass in grams numerically equal to the molecular mass in u, 44.0095 g/mol, i.e., 44.0095 g contains N_A CO_2 molecules.

Many common substances are ionic, e.g., sodium chloride, NaCl. A crystal of NaCl contains sodium ions, Na$^+$, and chloride ions, Cl$^-$, arranged in a regular spatial array. Although there are no NaCl molecules, the formula indicates the relative number of atoms of each element present in the crystal, and we can speak of the molar mass of NaCl, $22.98977 + 35.4527 = 58.4425$ g/mol, as the mass of sodium chloride which contains N_A sodium ions and N_A chloride ions. We also speak of the molar mass of an ion, e.g., OH$^-$, $15.9994 + 1.00794 = 17.0073$ g/mol, as the mass of N_A hydroxide ions.

Older books and chemical journals used the terms *atomic weight* and *molecular weight* rather than *atomic mass* and *molar mass*. Because "weight" is a force rather than a mass, such usage is potentially confusing and is now discouraged, but many chemists trained in an earlier time still use the old terms, so you may encounter them.

Don't Forget

Atomic mass refers to the mass of one mole of an element. Molar mass refers to the mass of one mole of molecules, formula units, or ions.

Empirical Formula from Composition

An empirical formula expresses the relative numbers of atoms of the different elements in a compound using the smallest integers possible. These integers are found by converting mass composition data to the moles of each element contained in some fixed mass of the compound. Consider a compound that contains 17.09% Mg, 37.93% Al, and 44.98% O. (Unless otherwise stated, percentage is a *mass* percentage, i.e., grams of the element per 100 g of the compound.) A systematic scheme for handing the data is shown in Table 2-2.

Table 2-2

(1) Element E	(2) Mass E in 100 g cmpd. $m(E)$	(3) Atomic mass $A_r(E)$	(4) Moles E in 100 g cmpd. $n(E) = \dfrac{m(E)}{A_r(E)}$	(5) Mole ratios $\dfrac{n(E)}{n_{min}(E)}$
Mg	17.09 g	24.31 g/mol	0.703 mol	1.00
Al	37.93 g	26.98 g/mol	1.406 mol	2.00
O	44.98 g	16.00 g/mol	2.812 mol	4.00

The numbers in column (4) are the numbers of moles of atoms of the component elements in 100 g of compound. The numbers in column (5) are obtained by dividing each $n(E)$ by the *smallest* $n(E)$, 0.703. Thus the relative numbers of moles of atoms of Mg, Al, and O are 1:2:4, and the empirical formula is $MgAl_2O_4$.

Tables 2-2 and 2-3 summarize the procedure for determining an empirical formula from composition data and vice versa.

The existence of a formula for a compound implies that a fixed relationship exists between the masses of any two elements in the compound or between the mass of any element and the mass of the compound as a whole. These relationships can be seen by writing the formula in vertical form, as illustrated in Table 2-3 for Al_2O_3.

Column (4) shows the masses of the elements contained in 1 mol of Al_2O_3; the sum is the molar mass of the compound. The entries in column (5) represent the *fractional* content of the various elements in the compound. These numbers are dimensionless (g/g), and when multiplied by 100%, represent the mass percentages of aluminum and oxygen in Al_2O_3, 52.9 and 47.1%, respectively. The sum of the constituent percentages of any compound must equal 100.0%.

Table 2-3

(1)	(2) $n(E)$	(3) $A_r(E)$	(4) $n(E) \times A_r(E)$	(5) $m(E)$ per g cmpd.
2 Al	2 mol	27.0 g/mol	54.0 g	$\dfrac{54.0 \text{ g Al}}{102.0 \text{ g Al}_2\text{O}_3} = 0.529$
3 O	3 mol	16.0 g/mol	48.0 g	$\dfrac{48.0 \text{ g O}}{102.0 \text{ g Al}_2\text{O}_3} = 0.471$
Al_2O_3	1 mol	102.0		Check: 1.000

Pure aluminum oxide always contains 52.9% Al, 47.1% O, an example of the *Law of Definite Proportions*. This empirical law applies to almost all chemical compounds and was of great importance in the acceptance of Dalton's atomic theory.

Not all chemical species obey the law of definite proportions. Systems which obey the law, i.e., those which have fixed ratios of atoms, are compounds. Systems which do not have fixed composition are called *mixtures*. Liquid solutions and metal alloys such as brass (copper, zinc, and lead) are common examples of mixtures.

Another law of historical importance, the *Law of Multiple Proportions*, states that the relative amounts of an element combining with a fixed amount of a second element in a series of compounds are the ratios of small whole numbers. For example, three oxides of nitrogen contain 63.65% N (A), 46.68% N (B), and 30.45% N (C). Table 2-4 shows the mass of N and the mass of O contained in 100 g of each compound, and the ratios, m_N/m_O:

Table 2-4

	A	B	C
m_N	63.65	46.68	30.45
m_O	36.35	53.32	69.55
m_N/m_O	1.7510	0.8755	0.4378

The last row of the table shows the mass of N per gram of O. The ratios of these numbers are:

$$\frac{1.7510}{0.4378} : \frac{0.8755}{0.4378} : \frac{0.4378}{0.4378} = 4.000 : 2.000 : 1.000$$

and, sure enough, ratios of small whole numbers are obtained.

The law of multiple proportions, in its historical form, is somewhat confusing, but we can understand it better by determining the empirical formulas of the nitrogen oxides. Following the procedure of Table 2-2, we convert the masses of N and O contained in 100 g of each compound to moles as shown in Table 2-5. The mole ratios then indicate the relative numbers of N and O atoms in one molecule:

Table 2-5

$A_r(E)$		A	B	C
14.01 g/mol N	mol N/100 g cmpd	4.544	3.333	2.174
16.00 g/mol O	mol O/100 g cmpd	2.272	3.333	4.347
	mol N/mol O	2.000	1.000	0.5000

The empirical formulas are A = N_2O, B = NO and C = NO_2. Thus the law of multiple proportions is just an example of molecules containing integral numbers of atoms of the constituent elements.

Chemical Formulas from Mass Spectrometry

The molecular mass of a compound is the average mass (in u) of a molecule, weighted among the various isotopic forms (*isotopomers*) of the different component elements. A nuclidic molecular mass may be defined for a molecule made up of particular nuclides by adding nuclidic atomic masses in the same way that the molecular mass is computed from average atomic masses.

A *mass spectrometer* is an instrument that separates particles by mass and measures their individual relative masses. If a nuclidic mass of an unknown compound is known with great precision from mass spectrometry, the exact molecular formula can often be deduced directly from this information without resort to a quantitative chemical analysis.

Example 1. Consider carbon monoxide, CO, dinitrogen, N_2, and ethylene, C_2H_4. The masses and fractional abundances of some isotopic forms of these molecules are listed in Table 2-6 (isotopic forms not listed have abundances less than 0.0001 or 0.01%). Since ^{12}C, ^{16}O, ^{14}N, and ^1H are by far the most abundant isotopes of C, O, N, and H, a particle of mass number 28 will be detected in all three cases. With a mass spectrum, Figure 2-1, the three gases can be distinguished on the basis of their nuclidic masses. The mass 29 and 30 satellites provide confirmation of the assignment.

Table 2-6

Mass No.	Isotopomer	Fraction	Mass/u
28	$^{12}C^{16}O$	0.9865	27.99491
	$^{14}N_2$	0.9928	28.00614
	$^{12}C_2{}^1H_4$	0.9773	28.03132
29	$^{13}C^{16}O$	0.0110	28.99823
	$^{12}C^{17}O$	0.0004	28.99913
	$^{14}N^{15}N$	0.0072	29.00318
	$^{12}C^{13}C^1H_4$	0.0219	29.03467
	$^{12}C_2{}^1H_3{}^2H$	0.0006	29.03759
30	$^{12}C^{18}O$	0.0020	29.99916
	$^{13}C_2{}^1H_4$	0.0001	30.03802

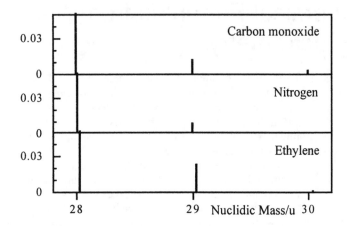

Figure 2-1. Mass spectra of CO, N_2, and C_2H_4. Note that the major peak at mass 28 has been truncated.

Example 2. Find the formula of an organic compound whose dominant nuclidic species has a precise nuclidic molecular mass of 44.025 u, given that no other elements than C, H, O, and N are present and only ^{12}C, ^1H, ^{16}O, and ^{14}N are involved.

Considering all possible combinations of C, H, O, and N, we find six molecular formulas with nuclidic molecular masses of about 44. These are listed in Table 2-7 with nuclidic molecular masses.

Table 2-7

Molecular formula	Nuclidic molecular mass	Molecular formula	Nuclidic molecular mass
C_3H_8	44.063 u	CH_4N_2	44.037 u
C_2H_4O	44.026 u	CH_2ON	44.014 u
C_2H_6N	44.050 u	CO_2	43.990 u

When these nuclidic masses are compared with the experimental value, 44.025 u, C_2H_4O is the only formula that fits the data within the claimed precision; so this must be the formula of the compound.

Problems

2.1   Given data in Table 2-1, compute the average atomic mass of C.
Ans. 12.011 u

2.2   A 1.5276-g sample of $CdCl_2$ was converted to metallic cadmium and cadmium-free products by electrolysis. The weight of the metallic cadmium was 0.9367 g. If $A_r(Cl) = 35.453$ u, what is $A_r(Cd)$?
Ans. 112.4 u

2.3   How many (a) grams of H_2S, (b) moles of H and of S, (c) grams of H and of S, (d) molecules of H_2S are contained in 0.400 mol H_2S?   *Ans.* (a) 13.63 g H_2S, (b) 0.800 mol H, 0.400 mol S, (c) 0.806 g H, 13.83 g S,(d) 2.41 × 10²³ molecules

2.4   A borane (containing only B and H) contained 88.45% B. What is its empirical formula?
Ans. B_5H_7

2.5   Determine the percentage composition of potassium carbonate, K_2CO_3.   *Ans.* 56.58% K, 8.69% C, 34.73% O

2.6   Pyrex glass typically contains 12.9% B_2O_3, 2.2% Al_2O_3, 3.8% Na_2O, 0.4% K_2O, and 80.7% SiO_2. What is the ratio of silicon to boron atoms in the glass?
Ans. 3.6

2.7   An element X forms four oxides containing 77.4, 63.2, 69.6, and 72.0% X. If the compound with 77.4% X is XO, what is X, and what are the empirical formulas of the other compounds?
Ans. X = Mn; MnO_2, Mn_2O_3, and Mn_3O_4

2.8   A sample of impure cuprite, Cu_2O, contains 66.6% copper. Assuming that the impurities do not contain copper, what percentage of the sample is Cu_2O?
Ans. 75.0% Cu_2O

2.9   The dominant peak in the mass spectrum of an organic compound gave a nuclidic molecular mass of 117.090 u. If it was known in advance that the compound contained only C, H, and O and that no more than four oxygen atoms are present in the molecule, what is its molecular formula?
Ans. $C_6H_{13}O_2$

2.10   An organic compound was prepared containing at least one and no more than two sulfur atoms per molecule. The compound had C and H, no N, but O could have been present. The molecular mass of the predominant nuclidic species was 110.020 u, as determined by mass spectrometry. What is the molecular formula of the compound?
Ans. C_6H_6S

Chapter 3
CALCULATIONS BASED ON CHEMICAL EQUATIONS

IN THIS CHAPTER:

✔ *Balancing Chemical Equations*
✔ *Types of Chemical Reactions*
✔ *Mass Relations from Equations*

Balancing Chemical Equations

A balanced equation is the basis for all calculations of the quantities of substances involved in a chemical reaction. In the course of balancing equations and working the related numerical problems, the alert student will not only develop skill in calculation, but will acquire much knowledge of descriptive and practical chemistry.

When substances—the *reactants*—react to form new substances—the *products*—we say that a chemical reaction has occurred. A chemical equation is a statement of such an event in which the formulas of the reactants are on the left, followed by a right-pointing arrow and then the formulas of the products. In a *balanced equation*, coefficients specify the number of molecules (or formula units) of each species involved. The coefficients must satisfy Dalton's requirement that atoms are not created or destroyed in a chemical reaction. There is no fixed procedure for balancing an equation. Although a systematic algebraic approach is in principle possible, a trial-and-error approach often works.

Example 1. Balance: $FeS_2(s) + O_2(g) \rightarrow Fe_2O_3(s) + SO_2(g)$

We start with an algebraic approach, writing the unknown integral coefficients as w, x, y and z:

$$w\ FeS_2 + x\ O_2 \rightarrow y\ Fe_2O_3 + z\ SO_2$$

Dalton's rule leads to conservation relations for Fe, S and O:

$\quad$ Fe: $w = 2y$ $\qquad$ S: $2w = z$ $\qquad$ O: $2x = 3y + 2z$

Since $2x$ and $2z$ are necessarily even numbers, we see that y must also be even; let us guess $y = 2$. The three equations then give $w = 4$, $z = 8$, and $x = 11$. The complete equation then is

$$4\ FeS_2 + 11\ O_2 \rightarrow 2\ Fe_2O_3 + 8\ SO_2$$

The trial-and-error approach also works well. We can start by focusing on one element, say Fe. Since Fe_2O_3 has two Fe atoms, we can set the coefficient of FeS_2 to 2, obtaining

$$2\ FeS_2 + O_2 \rightarrow Fe_2O_3 + SO_2$$

Next we balance S; since $2\ FeS_2$ contains 4 S atoms, the coefficient of SO_2 must be 4

$$2\ FeS_2 + O_2 \rightarrow Fe_2O_3 + 4\ SO_2$$

Finally we balance O. The right-hand side has $3 + 8 = 11$ O atoms. The equation could be balanced by using a coefficient $11/2$ for O_2, but since we want integral coefficients, we multiply through by 2 to obtain the same result obtained by the algebraic approach.

Example 2. Balance: $C_7H_6O_2(s) + O_2(g) \rightarrow CO_2(g) + H_2O(l)$

This time, we use the trial-and-error approach. With 7 C on the left, we must have 7 on the right:

$$C_7H_6O_2 + O_2 \rightarrow 7\ CO_2 + H_2O$$

With 6 H on the left, we must have 6 on the right:

$$C_7H_6O_2 + O_2 \rightarrow 7\ CO_2 + 3\ H_2O$$

We now have $7 \times 2 + 3 = 17$ O atoms on the right which, in view of 2 O atoms in $C_7H_6O_2$, suggests a coefficient $15/2$ for O_2 on the left. Again multiplying through by 2, we have

$$2\ C_7H_6O_2 + 15\ O_2 \rightarrow 14\ CO_2 + 6\ H_2O$$

Key Rule for Balancing Equations:

Atoms are neither created nor destroyed in a chemical equation.

Types of Chemical Reactions

Skill in balancing equations will increase rapidly with practice, especially as you learn to recognize common types of reactions. Recognition of the reaction type often helps in the prediction of the products of the reaction, if they are not stated. A few examples of the more predictable types are given below.

Combustion reactions. Oxygen in excess (usually from the air) combines with organic compounds (containing C, H, and sometimes O) to produce carbon dioxide (CO_2) and water (H_2O), e.g.,

$$C_2H_6O(l) + 3\ O_2(g) \rightarrow 2\ CO_2(g) + 3\ H_2O(l)$$

Organic compounds containing nitrogen or sulfur also burn in air to produce CO_2 and H_2O, but the nitrogen and sulfur oxides produced depend on the temperature and oxygen pressure.

Replacement reactions. A more active element replaces a less active one in a compound, e.g.,

$$Zn(s) + CuSO_4(aq) \rightarrow Cu(s) + ZnSO_4(aq)$$

$$2\ Mg(s) + TiCl_4(l) \rightarrow Ti(s) + 2\ MgCl_2(s)$$

Double displacement reactions (**metathesis**). Particularly common for ionic reactions in solution, atoms or groups of atoms "exchange partners" if an insoluble salt results, e.g.,

$$AgNO_3(aq) + NaCl(aq) \rightarrow NaNO_3(aq) + AgCl(s)$$

$$BaCl_2(aq) + Na_2SO_4(aq) \rightarrow 2\ NaCl(aq) + BaSO_4(s)$$

Acid-base reactions (**neutralization**). An acid, which contributes H^+, and a base, which contributes OH^-, undergo metathesis to produce water and a salt, e.g.,

$$HCl(aq) + NaOH(aq) \rightarrow NaCl(aq) + H_2O(l)$$

$$H_2SO_4(aq) + Mg(OH)_2(aq) \rightarrow MgSO_4(aq) + 2\ H_2O(l)$$

The following two reaction types unfortunately afford no simple ways to predict the products.

Combination reactions. Elements or compounds simply combine to form one product, e.g.,

$$2\ SO_2(g) + O_2(g) \rightarrow 2\ SO_3(g)$$

$$P_4(s) + 6\ Cl_2(g) \rightarrow 4\ PCl_3(g)$$

or $$P_4(s) + 10\ Cl_2(g) \rightarrow 4\ PCl_5(g)$$

Products of the reaction of P_4 and Cl_2 depend on the ratio of reactants and the conditions of temperature and pressure.

Decomposition reactions. A single reactant is transformed by heat or electrolysis into two or more products, e.g.,

(electrolysis) $\quad 2 H_2O(l) \rightarrow 2 H_2(g) + O_2(g)$

(heat) $\quad 2 HgO(s) \rightarrow 2 Hg(l) + O_2(g)$

or $\quad 4 HgO(s) \rightarrow 2 Hg_2O(s) + O_2(g)$

Products of the decomposition of HgO depend on the temperature and oxygen pressure.

Mass Relations from Equations

The *relative numbers* of reactant and product molecules (or the relative numbers of moles) are indicated by the coefficients of a balanced chemical equation. Using molar masses, we can compute the relative masses of reactants and products in a chemical reaction.

Example 3. Ammonia reacts with oxygen according to the equation

$$4 NH_3(g) + 3 O_2(g) \rightarrow 2 N_2(g) + 6 H_2O(l)$$

Thus 4 moles of NH_3 react with 3 moles of O_2 to form 2 moles of N_2 and 6 moles of H_2O. Suppose that the reaction consumes 10.00 g NH_3. This corresponds to

$$n(NH_3) = \frac{10.00 \text{ g}}{17.03 \text{ g/mol}} = 0.5872 \text{ mol } NH_3$$

From the mole ratios, the reaction must involve

$$n(O_2) = 3/4 \times 0.5872 = 0.4404 \text{ mol } O_2$$
$$n(N_2) = 2/4 \times 0.5872 = 0.2936 \text{ mol } N_2$$
$$n(H_2O) = 6/4 \times 0.5872 = 0.8808 \text{ mol } H_2O$$

Using the molar masses, we can compute the mass of O_2 reacting and the masses of N_2 and H_2O produced:

$$m(O_2) = 0.4404 \text{ mol} \times 32.00 \text{ g/mol} = 14.09 \text{ g } O_2$$
$$m(N_2) = 0.2936 \text{ mol} \times 28.01 \text{ g/mol} = 8.22 \text{ g } N_2$$
$$m(H_2O) = 0.8808 \text{ mol} \times 18.02 \text{ g/mol} = 15.87 \text{ g } H_2O$$

Notice that mass is conserved (as required) in the reaction:

$$10.00 \text{ g } NH_3 + 14.09 \text{ g } O_2 = 8.22 \text{ g } N_2 + 15.87 \text{ g } H_2O$$

Often a problem gives the mass of one reactant or product and you are to determine the masses of the other substances involved. In problems of this kind, you may assume that sufficient amounts of the other reactants are present. If the masses of *two* reactants are given, you must

> # Summary of Mass Relations:
>
> - Mass is conserved in a chemical reaction.
> - Mass relations do not depend on the phase of a reactant or product species, e.g., whether H_2O is liquid water or steam.
> - Mass relations do not require knowledge of true molecular formulas. They are equally valid for empirical and molecular formulas, for molecules which may dissociate—S_8, P_4, N_2O_4, I_2, etc.—or polymerize—starch, cellulose, etc.

determine which one (if either) is in excess. The best approach is to convert the given masses to moles and compare the mole ratio to that determined by the balanced equation.

Example 4. A solution containing 2.00 g of $Hg(NO_3)_2$ was added to a solution containing 2.00 g of Na_2S. Calculate the mass of products formed according to the reaction

$$Hg(NO_3)_2(aq) + Na_2S(aq) \rightarrow HgS(s) + 2\ NaNO_3(aq)$$

We begin by calculating the number of moles of each reactant:

$$n\left[Hg(NO_3)_2\right] = \frac{2.00\ g}{324.6\ g/mol} = 6.16 \times 10^{-3}\ mol$$

$$n\left[Na_2S\right] = \frac{2.00\ g}{78.00\ g/mol} = 2.56 \times 10^{-2}\ mol$$

The equation indicates that equimolar quantities of reactants are required. Hence the given amount of $Hg_2(NO_3)_2$ requires only 6.16×10^{-3} mol of Na_2S. Thus 1.94×10^{-2} mol (1.51 g) of Na_2S remains unreacted. $Hg_2(NO_3)_2$ is the *limiting reagent* and we expect to form 6.16 $\times 10^{-3}$ mol HgS and $2(6.16 \times 10^{-3}) = 1.23 \times 10^{-2}$ mol $NaNO_3$:

$$m(HgS) = \left(6.16 \times 10^{-3} \text{ mol HgS}\right)\left(\frac{232.6 \text{ g HgS}}{1 \text{ mol HgS}}\right)$$

$$= 1.43\text{g HgS}$$

$$m(NaNO_3) = \left(1.23 \times 10^{-2} \text{ mol NaNO}_3\right)\left(\frac{85.0 \text{ g NaNO}_3}{1 \text{ mol NaNO}_3}\right)$$

$$= 1.05 \text{ g NaNO}_3$$

In summary, the original 4.00 g of reagents has been transformed to 1.43 g HgS and 1.05 g $NaNO_3$ with 1.51 g Na_2S unreacted. Note that the sum of the final masses is 3.99 g, within round-off error of the original 4.00 g.

Problems

3.1 Balance the following equations:
(a) $C_2H_4(OH)_2(s) + O_2(g) \rightarrow CO_2(g) + H_2O(l)$
(b) $Li(s) + H_2O(l) \rightarrow LiOH(aq) + H_2(g)$
(c) $Ba(OH)_2(aq) + AlCl_3(aq) \rightarrow BaCl_2(aq) + Al(OH)_3(s)$
(d) $KHC_8H_4O_4(aq) + KOH(aq) \rightarrow K_2C_8H_4O_4(aq) + H_2O(l)$
(e) $(NH_4)_2Cr_2O_7(s) \rightarrow N_2(g) + Cr_2O_3(s) + H_2O(g)$
Ans. Coefficients are (a) 2, 5, 4, 6; (b) 2, 2, 2, 1;
(c) 3, 2, 3, 2; (d) 1, 1, 1, 1; (e) 1, 1, 1, 4

3.2 Predict the products of the following reactions and balance the equation:
(a) $HCl(aq) + Mg(OH)_2(s) \rightarrow$ *Ans.* $2 H_2O(l) + MgCl_2(aq)$
(b) $PbCl_2(aq) + K_2SO_4(aq) \rightarrow$ *Ans.* $PbSO_4(s) + 2 KCl(aq)$
(c) $CH_3CH_2OH(l) + O_2(g) \rightarrow$ *Ans.* $2 CO_2(g) + 3 H_2O(l)$
(d) $Fe(s) + AgNO_3(aq) \rightarrow$ *Ans.* $2 Ag(s) + Fe(NO_3)_2(aq)$

3.3 Consider the combustion of amyl alcohol, $C_5H_{11}OH$:

$$2 C_5H_{11}OH(l) + 15 O_2(g) \rightarrow 10 CO_2(g) + 12 H_2O(l)$$

(a) How many moles of O_2 are needed for the combustion of 1 mole of amyl alcohol? (b) How many moles of H_2O are formed for each mole of O_2 consumed? (c) How many grams of CO_2 are produced for each mole of amyl alcohol burned? (d) How many grams of CO_2 are produced for each gram of amyl alcohol burned? (e) How many tons of CO_2 are produced for each ton of amyl alcohol burned?

Ans. (a) 7.5 mol O_2, (b) 0.80 mol H_2O, (c) 220 g CO_2
(d) 2.50 g CO_2, (e) 2.50 tons CO_2

3.4 A portable hydrogen generator utilizes the reaction
$$CaH_2(s) + 2\ H_2O(l) \rightarrow Ca(OH)_2(s) + 2\ H_2(g)$$
How many grams of H_2 can be produced by 50 g of CaH_2?

Ans. 4.8 g H_2

3.5 How much iron(III) oxide can be produced from 6.76 g of $FeCl_3 \cdot 6H_2O$ by the following reactions?
$$FeCl_3 \cdot 6H_2O(s) + 3\ NH_3(g) \rightarrow Fe(OH)_3(s) + 3\ NH_4Cl(s)$$
$$2\ Fe(OH)_3(s) \rightarrow Fe_2O_3(s) + 3\ H_2O(g) \qquad Ans.\ 2.00\ g\ Fe_2O_3$$

3.6 In a rocket motor fueled with butane, C_4H_{10}, how many kilograms of liquid oxygen should be provided with each kilogram of butane to provide for complete combustion?

Ans. 3.58 kg

3.7 A mixture of 100 g Al and 200 g MnO was heated to initiate the reaction, $2\ Al(s) + 3\ MnO(s) \rightarrow Al_2O_3(s) + 3\ Mn(s)$. Which initial substance remained in excess? How much? *Ans.* 49 g Al

3.8 Ethyl alcohol, C_2H_5OH, can be made by the fermentation of glucose, $C_6H_{12}O_6$, as indicated by the (unbalanced) equation:
$$C_6H_{12}O_6(aq) \rightarrow C_2H_5OH(aq) + CO_2(g)$$
How many metric tons of alcohol can be made from 2.00 metric tons of glucose? *Ans.* 1.02 metric tons

3.9 In the Mond process for purifying nickel, the volatile nickel carbonyl, $Ni(CO)_4$, is produced by the reaction:
$$Ni(s) + 4\ CO(g) \rightarrow Ni(CO)_4(g)$$
How much CO is used in volatilizing each kilogram of nickel?

Ans. 1.91 kg CO

3.10 A mixture of 1 ton of CS_2 and 2 tons of Cl_2 is passed through a hot reaction tube, where the following reaction takes place:
$$CS_2(g) + 3\ Cl_2(g) \rightarrow CCl_4(l) + S_2Cl_2(l)$$
(a) How much CCl_4 can be made by complete reaction of the limiting starting material? (b) Which starting material is in excess, and how much of it remains unreacted?

Ans. (a) 1.45 tons CCl_4, (b) 0.28 ton CS_2

3.11 What mass of Cu_2S can be produced from the reaction of 100 g copper with 50 g of sulfur? *Ans.* 125 g Cu_2S

Chapter 4
CONCENTRATION AND SOLUTION STOICHIOMETRY

IN THIS CHAPTER:

✔ *Measures of Concentration*
✔ *Stoichiometry of Reactions in Solution*

Introduction

In a liquid solution, the dissolved substance is called the *solute*, the liquid in which the solute is dissolved is the *solvent*. Usually the distinction is clear and unambiguous, e.g., in an aqueous solution of NaCl, sodium chloride is the solute, water the solvent. In a mixture of two liquids, e.g., water and methanol, CH_3OH, the designation of solvent and solute may be entirely arbitrary.

Measures of Concentration

Measures of solution composition commonly used in chemistry:

Mass Percent Composition. Solution composition can be specified by the mass percents of solute and solvent. Thus a 10% aqueous solution of NaCl contains 10 g of NaCl and 90 g of H_2O to form 100 g of solution.

Molal Concentration. The number of moles of solute per kilogram of solvent is defined as the molal concentration or *molality*.

Molar Concentration. The number of moles of solute per liter of solution is defined as the molar concentration or *molarity*. We usually write the molar concentration of NaCl as [NaCl] or C_{NaCl}. Since sodium chloride is completely dissociated into Na^+ and Cl^- ions in aqueous solution, $[NaCl] = [Na^+] = [Cl^-]$.

Mole Fractions. Solution composition can also be described by the number of moles of solute and solvent. The mole fraction of a solution component, then, is the ratio of the number of moles of that component divided by the total number of moles. We could multiply a mole fraction by 100% and speak of mole %, but we usually avoid this usage to avoid confusion with mass %. Thus if a solution is described in terms of % composition, you can assume mass %.

Remember

Measures of Solution Composition:

$$\% \text{ mass} = \frac{\text{mass solute}}{\text{mass solution}} \times 100\%$$

$$\text{mole fraction} = X_A = \frac{\text{moles A}}{\text{total number of moles}}$$

$$\text{molarity of A} = C_A = [A] = \frac{\text{moles A}}{\text{solution volume in L}}$$

$$\text{molarity of A} = m_A = \frac{\text{moles A}}{\text{solvent mass in kg}}$$

Interconversion of Composition Measures. Given the solution composition in mass percent, it is easy to compute the mole fractions of solute and solvent and the molal concentration of solute.

Example 1. What are the mole fractions and molal concentrations in a 10% by weight solution of CH_3OH in water?

We first compute the number of moles of CH_3OH and water:

$$n_{CH_3OH} = \frac{10.0 \text{ g } CH_3OH}{32.05 \text{ g/mol}} = 0.312 \text{ mol}$$

$$n_{H_2O} = \frac{90.0 \text{ g } H_2O}{18.02 \text{ g/mol}} = 4.99 \text{ mol}$$

The total number of moles is 5.33 and the mole fractions are:

$$X_{CH_3OH} = \frac{0.312 \text{ mol } CH_3OH}{5.30 \text{ mol}} = 0.0589$$

$$X_{H_2O} = \frac{4.99 \text{ mol } H_2O}{5.30 \text{ mol}} = 0.941$$

The molal concentrations of CH_3OH is computed from the number of moles and the mass of H_2O.

$$m_{CH_3OH} = \frac{0.312 \text{ mol}}{90 \times 10^{-3} \text{ kg } H_2O} = 3.47 \text{ mol/kg}$$

Molar concentrations involve the volume of the solution and to get this from the mass, we need the density.

Example 2. Given that the density of 10.0% aqueous NaCl is 1.071 g/cm^3, what is the molar concentrations of Na^+ and Cl^-?

Two approaches are possible. (1) We know how many moles of NaCl are contained in 100 g of solution. Thus we have

$$n_{NaCl} = \frac{10.0 \text{ g NaCl}}{58.44 \text{ g/mol}} = 0.171 \text{ mol}$$

$$[Na^+] = [Cl^-] = \left(\frac{0.171 \text{ mol NaCl}}{100 \text{ g solution}}\right)\left(\frac{1.071 \text{ g}}{cm^3 \text{ soln.}}\right)\left(\frac{1000 \text{ cm}^3}{L}\right) = 1.83 \text{ mol/L}$$

(2) One liter of solution weighs 1071 g and contains 107.1 g NaCl/L; converting to moles, we have $[NaCl] = [Na^+] = [Cl^-] = 1.83$ mol/L.

Dilution Problems. If a solution is diluted, the volume is increased and the concentration of solute decreased, but the number of moles of solute remains constant. Since $C = n/V$, $n = CV$, and we have a simple relation between the original molar concentration and volume and the final concentration and volume after dilution:

$$C_1V_1 = C_2V_2$$

The subscripts here refer to the particular state of the system, $_1$ to the initial state, and $_2$ to the final state

Example 3. Suppose that 25mL of the 1.83 M NaCl solution is diluted to 100 mL. What is the final molar concentration of NaCl?

$$C_2 = \frac{C_1 V_1}{V_1} = \frac{(25\ \text{mL})(1.83\ \text{mol}/\text{L})}{100\ \text{mL}} = 0.46\ \text{mol}/\text{L}$$

Comparison of the Concentration Scales. The molar concentration scale is most appropriate in *volumetric experiments* using pipets, volumetric flasks, and burets. A disadvantage of this scale is that molar concentrations are temperature-dependent since solution density depends (usually weakly) on temperature.

Concentrations expressed as molality or mole fractions are temperature-independent and are most useful when a physical measurement is related to theory over a range of temperature, e.g., in freezing point depression or boiling point elevation measurements (Chapter 11). Since the density of water is close to 1 g/cm^3, molal and molar concentrations are nearly equal numerically for dilute aqueous solutions (< 0.1 M).

Stoichiometry of Reactions in Solution

Stoichiometric calculations involving solutions of specified molar concentration are usually quite simple since the number of moles of a reactant or product is simply volume $\times$ molar concentration.

Example 4. What volume of 1.40 M H$_2$SO$_4$ is needed to react exactly with 100 g of aluminum according to the equation

$$2\ \text{Al(s)} + 3\ \text{H}_2\text{SO}_4\text{(aq)} \rightarrow \text{Al}_2(\text{SO}_4)_3 + 3\ \text{H}_2\text{(g)}?$$

First calculate the number of moles of Al, then moles of H$_2$SO$_4$ needed and then the volume of H$_2$SO$_4$ solution required:

$$n_{Al} = \frac{100\ \text{g Al}}{27.0\ \text{g}/\text{mol}} = 3.70\ \text{mol}$$

$$n_{H_2SO_4} = (3.70 \text{ mol Al}) \times \left(\frac{3 \text{ mol H}_2\text{SO}_4}{2 \text{ mol Al}} \right) = 5.55 \text{ mol}$$

$$V_{H_2SO_4} = \frac{5.55 \text{ mol H}_2\text{SO}_4}{1.40 \text{ mol/L}} = 3.96 \text{ L}$$

Example 5. 40.0 mL of an H_2SO_4 solution were titrated with 0.215 M NaOH. 35.26 mL of base was required to exactly neutralize H_2SO_4. What was the concentration of the acid?

The titration reaction,

$$H_2SO_4(aq) + 2 \text{ OH}^-(aq) \rightarrow SO_4^{2-}(aq) + 2 \text{ H}_2O(liq)$$

shows that 2 mol NaOH are needed to react with 1 mol H_2SO_4. Thus,

$$[H_2SO_4] = \frac{(0.215 \text{ mol/L})(35.26\text{mL NaOH})}{(2 \text{ mol NaOH/mol H}_2\text{SO}_4)(40.0 \text{ mL H}_2\text{SO}_4)} = .0948 \text{ M}$$

Problems

4.1 What are the molar concentrations of the Ba^{2+} and NO_3^- ions in a solution containing 37.5 g $Ba(NO_3)_2$ per liter?
Ans. 0.143 M Ba^{2+}, 0.286 M NO_3^-

4.2 A solution contains 20.0 g of sucrose, $C_{12}H_{22}O_{11}$, and 125 g H_2O. (a) What is the molality of sucrose? (b) What is the mole fraction of sucrose?
Ans. (a) 0.468 mol/kg, (b) 0.00834

4.3 What volume of 2.00 M $Pb(NO_3)_2$ contains 600 mg of lead?
Ans. 1.45 mL

4.4 A 4.51 g sample of an unknown compound was dissolved in 98.0 g of solvent. From the freezing point depression, the concentration was found to be 0.388 mol/kg. Calculate the molar mass of the unknown.
Ans. 119 g/mol

4.5 48.4 mL of a HCl solution is required to react with 1.240 g of pure $CaCO_3$ to produce $CO_2(g)$. What is the molarity of the acid?
Ans. 0.512 M

4.6 What volume of 5.00 M H_2SO_4 is required to neutralize a solution containing 2.50 g NaOH?
Ans. 6.25 mL

4.7 40.0 mL of 0.225 M $AgNO_3$ solution was required to react exactly with 25.0 mL of a solution of NaCN, according to the equation, $Ag^+(aq) + 2 \text{ CN}^-(aq) \rightarrow Ag(CN)_2^-(aq)$. What is the molar concentration of the NaCN solution?
Ans. 0.72 M

Chapter 5
THE IDEAL GAS LAW AND KINETIC THEORY

IN THIS CHAPTER:

✔ *Pressure*

✔ *Gas Laws*

✔ *Partial Pressures and Mole Fractions*

✔ *Reaction Stoichiometry Involving Gases*

✔ *The Kinetic Theory of Gases*

Pressure

Pressure is defined as the force acting on a unit area of surface

$$\text{Pressure} = \frac{\text{force acting perpendicular to an area}}{\text{area over which the force is distributed}}$$

$$\text{Pressure (in pascals)} = \frac{\text{force (in newtons)}}{\text{area (in square meters)}}$$

Thus 1 Pa = 1 N/m^2 = (1 kg m/s^2)/m^2 = 1 kg m^{-1}s^{-2}. In your study of chemistry, you will encounter several other pressure units. Some of these are listed in Table 5-1.

Table 5-1. Some Common Pressure Units

Pressure Unit	Definition
pascal (Pa)	1 Pa = 1 N/m^2
bar	1 bar = 10^5 Pa
atmosphere (atm)*	1 atm = 101325 Pa
	1 atm = 1.01325 bar
torr	760 torr = 1 atm
millimeter mercury (mm Hg)	1 mm Hg = 1 torr

* The average atmospheric pressure at sea level is approximately 1 atm.

The pressure exerted by a column of fluid is

Pressure = height × density of fluid × acceleration of gravity

Pressure (Pa) = height (m) × density (kg/m^3) × 9.80665 m/s^2

Example 1. What is the pressure at the bottom of a 2.00-m column of water (density 1.00 g/cm^3)? Express the pressure in Pa, bar, atm, and torr.

$$P = (2.00 \text{ m})\left(\frac{1.00 \text{ g}}{\text{cm}^3}\right)\left(\frac{10^{-3} \text{ kg}}{\text{g}}\right)\left(\frac{10^6 \text{ cm}^3}{\text{m}^3}\right)\left(\frac{9.81 \text{ m}}{\text{s}^2}\right)$$

$$= 1.96 \times 10^4 \frac{\text{kg m s}^2}{\text{s}^2} = 1.96 \times 10^4 \text{ N/m}^3 = 1.96 \times 10^4 \text{ Pa}$$

$$P = \frac{1.96 \times 10^4 \text{ Pa}}{10^5 \text{ Pa/bar}} = 0.196 \text{ bar}$$

$$P = \frac{0.196 \text{ bar}}{1.01325 \text{ bar/atm}} = 0.194 \text{ atm}$$

$$P = (0.194 \text{ atm})(760 \text{ torr/atm}) = 147 \text{ torr}$$

Gas Laws

At sufficiently low pressures and sufficiently high temperatures, all gases have been found to obey three empirical laws. These laws relate the volume of a gas to the temperature and pressure. When a gas obeys these three laws, it is said to behave as an *ideal gas* or *perfect gas*.

Boyle's law states that, at constant temperature and number of moles, the volume of a gas is inversely proportional to the volume:

$$PV = \text{constant} = f_1(n,T)$$

Charles' law states that at constant pressure and number of moles, the volume of a gas is proportional to the absolute temperature:

$$V = T \times f_2(n,P)$$

Gay-Lussac's law states that at constant volume and number of moles, the pressure of a gas is proportional to the absolute temperature:

$$P = T \times f_3(n,V)$$

There is ample experimental evidence, dating from the early 19th century, to say that the volume of a gas, at constant pressure and temperature, is proportional to the number of moles of gas. This observation is called *Avogadro's hypothesis*:

$$V = n \times f_4(P,T)$$

The three empirical laws and Avogadro's hypothesis are combined to give a single law, the *ideal gas law*:

$$\frac{PV}{nT} = R \text{ (a constant)} \quad \text{or} \quad PV = nRT \tag{5-1}$$

The constant R, called the *gas constant*, has the value

$$R = 8.3145 \text{ J mol}^{-1}\text{K}^{-1}$$

when all quantities in the ideal gas law are expressed in SI units—P in Pa, V in m^3, n in mol, and T in K. Alternatively if we express V in L, P in atm, n in mol, and T in K,

$$R = 0.08206 \text{ L atm mol}^{-1}\text{K}^{-1}$$

The ideal gas law is valid only for ideal gases. All gases can be liquefied at sufficiently high pressure and low temperature and gases become nonideal as they approach liquefaction. However, almost all gases behave nearly ideally at temperatures significantly above their boiling points and at pressures of a few atmospheres or less.

The ideal gas law, *PV = nRT,* is an *equation of state*. That is, given any three of the variables—*P, V, n,* and *T*—the fourth can be computed.

Example 2. What is the volume of 15.0 g of Ar at 90°C and 735 torr?

$$V = \frac{mRT}{MP} = \frac{(15.0 \text{ g})(0.0821 \text{ L atm mol}^{-1}\text{K}^{-1})(363 \text{ K})}{(39.9 \text{ g mol}^{-1})(735/760 \text{ atm})} = 11.6 \text{ L}$$

Example 3. 1.33 g of a gas occupied 560 cm³ at 1 atm, 298 K. How many moles are present? What is the molar mass?

$$n = \frac{PV}{RT} = \frac{(1.00 \text{ atm})(0.560 \text{ L})}{(0.0821 \text{ L atm mol}^{-1} \text{ K}^{-1})(298 \text{ K})} = 0.0229 \text{ mol}$$

$$M = \frac{m}{n} = \frac{1.33 \text{ g}}{0.0229 \text{ mol}} = 58.1 \text{ g/mol}$$

The ideal gas law allows us to compute the *molar volume* of an ideal gas, the volume occupied by one mole of gas:

$$\overline{V} = \frac{V}{n} = \frac{RT}{P} \tag{5-2}$$

At so-called *standard conditions of temperature and pressure (STP)*, 273 K and 1 atm, the molar volume is

$$\overline{V} = \frac{RT}{P} = \frac{(0.0821 \text{ L atm mol}^{-1} \text{ K}^{-1})(273 \text{ K})}{(1 \text{ atm})} = 22.4 \text{ L/mol}$$

For the *thermodynamic standard state*, 298 K and 1 atm, the molar volume is

$$\overline{V} = \frac{RT}{P} = \frac{(8.3145 \text{ J mol}^{-1} \text{ K}^{-1})(298 \text{ K})}{1.01325 \times 10^5 \text{ Pa}} = 0.0245 \text{ m}^3 \ (24.5 \text{ L})$$

The *density* of an ideal gas is closely related to the molar volume. Since $d = m/V$ and $m = nM$ (n = moles, M = molar mass in g/mol), we have

$$d = \frac{m}{V} = \frac{nM}{V} = \frac{MP}{RT} \tag{5-3}$$

Example 4. Compute the density of methane, CH_4, at 20°C and 2.00 atm.

$$d = \frac{MP}{RT} = \frac{(16.0 \text{ g/mol})(2.00 \text{ atm})}{(0.0821 \text{ L atm mol}^{-1}\text{K}^{-1})(293 \text{ K})} = 1.33 \text{ g/L}$$

Example 5. An organic compound containing 55.8% C, 7.03% H, and 37.2% O was found to have a gas density of 2.83 g/L at 100°C and 740 torr. What is the molecular formula of the compound?

Using the methods of Chapter 3, we find that the empirical formula is C_2H_3O. The gas density gives the molar mass:

$$M = \frac{dRT}{P} = \frac{(2.83 \text{ g/L})(0.0821 \text{ L atm mol}^{-1}\text{K}^{-1})(373 \text{ K})}{740/760 \text{ atm}} = 89.0 \text{ g/mol}$$

The empirical formula unit has a molar mass of 43.0 g/mol. The exact molar mass must therefore be $2 \times 43.0 = 86.0$ g/mol, which is reasonably close to the experimental result, 89.0 g/mol. The molecular formula must therefore be $C_4H_6O_2$.

Partial Pressures and Mole Fractions

A mixture of gases also obeys the ideal gas law (at sufficiently low total pressure and high temperature). For volume V, temperature T, and total number of moles, $n_{total} = n_1 + n_2 + n_3 + \bullet\bullet\bullet$, the total pressure is:

$$P_{total} = \frac{n_{total} RT}{V} = \frac{n_1 RT}{V} + \frac{n_2 RT}{V} + \frac{n_3 RT}{V} + \ldots \qquad (5\text{-}4)$$

which invites us to write $P_{total} = P_1 + P_2 + P_3 + \ldots$

where

$$P_i = \frac{n_i RT}{V} \qquad (5\text{-}5)$$

is called the *partial pressure* of component i.

The concept of partial pressures can also be understood in terms of the *mole fraction* of component i, defined as the ratio of the number of moles of component i to the total moles of gas,

$$X_i = \frac{n_i}{n_{total}} \qquad (5\text{-}6)$$

Since $P_i = n_i (RT/V)$ and $P_{total} = n_{total} (RT/V)$, we see that the mole fraction of component i can also be expressed by the ratio of the partial pressure of component i to the total pressure,

$$X_i = \frac{P_i}{P_{total}} \qquad (5\text{-}7)$$

Example 6. In a gas mixture, the partial pressure of H_2 is 200 torr, that of CO_2 is 150 torr, and that of CH_4 is 320 torr. What is the total pressure? What are the mole fractions of the three components?

$$P_{total} = 200 + 150 + 320 = 670 \text{ torr}$$

$$X_{H_2} = \frac{200 \text{ torr}}{670 \text{ torr}} = 0.29 \qquad X_{CO_2} = \frac{150 \text{ torr}}{670 \text{ torr}} = 0.224$$

$$X_{CH_4} = \frac{320 \text{ torr}}{670 \text{ torr}} = 0.478$$

Notice that the mole fractions sum to 1.000.

Example 7. 100 cm³ of oxygen is collected over liquid water at 23°C, at which temperature the vapor pressure of water is 21.1 torr. The pressure of the gas mixture is 800 torr. To what volume of pure O_2 at STP (273 K, 1 atm) does this amount correspond?

The gas collected is a mixture of O_2 and H_2O vapor and the partial pressure of H_2O is 21.1 torr. Thus the partial pressure of O_2 is 800 – 21.1 = 779 torr. Had the O_2 been pure, it would have occupied 100 cm³ at a pressure of 779 torr, 23 + 273 = 296 K. Converting to STP with $P_1V_1/T_1 = P_2V_2/T_2$,

$$V_2 = V_1 \left(\frac{T_2}{T_1}\right)\left(\frac{P_1}{P_2}\right) = \left(100 \text{ cm}^3\right)\left(\frac{273 \text{ K}}{296 \text{ K}}\right)\left(\frac{779 \text{ torr}}{760 \text{ torr}}\right) = 94.5 \text{ cm}^3$$

Reaction Stoichiometry Involving Gases

At constant temperature and pressure, V is proportional to n and thus to mass. In this way, the ideal gas law provides us with a connection to the mole/mass relations implied by a chemical equation.

Example 8. How many grams of zinc must be dissolved in sulfuric acid in order to produce 500 cm³ of hydrogen at 20°C and 770 torr?

$$Zn(s) + H_2SO_4(aq) \rightarrow ZnSO_4(aq) + H_2(g)$$

First find the number of moles of H_2 using the ideal gas law:

$$n = \frac{PV}{RT} = \frac{(770/760 \text{ atm})(0.500 \text{ L})}{(0.0821 \text{ L atm mol}^{-1}\text{K}^{-1})(293 \text{ K})} = 0.0211 \text{ mol H}_2$$

$$\left(0.0211 \text{ mol H}_2\right)\left(\frac{1 \text{ mol Zn}}{1 \text{ mol H}_2}\right)\left(\frac{65.4 \text{ g Zn}}{1 \text{ mol Zn}}\right) = 1.38 \text{ g Zn}$$

Don't Forget

In reaction stoichiometry problems involving gases, the ideal gas law provides a means to compute moles from pressure or volume data.

The Kinetic Theory of Gases

Boyle's law can be derived from theoretical principles by making a few assumptions about the nature of gases. In the process, we obtain an important insight into the nature of temperature.

Basic assumptions of kinetic theory:

1. A gas consists of a very large number of molecules of negligible size which are in a state of constant random motion. Pressure results from molecular collisions with the container walls.

2. Collisions between molecules or between a molecule and the walls of the container are perfectly elastic, i.e., there is no change in the molecular kinetic energy in a collision.

3. Intermolecular forces are negligible aside from collisions. Between collisions, a molecule travels in a straight line at constant speed.

4. The kinetic energy of a gas molecule is given by $E = mu^2/2$, where m and u are the molecular mass and speed, respectively.

Major predictions of kinetic theory:

(a) For a gas composed on N molecules,

$$PV = \frac{2}{3}NE_{average} = \frac{2}{3}N\left(\frac{1}{2}mu^2\right)_{average}$$

Comparing this with the ideal gas law, we have with $N = nN_A$:

$$\frac{2}{3}NE_{average} = nRT \qquad E_{average} = \frac{3}{2}\frac{R}{N_A}T = \frac{3}{2}kT$$

(5-8)

where $k = R/N_A$, Boltzmann's constant, may be thought of as the gas constant per molecule.

(b) The distribution of speeds over the assemblage of molecules is given by an the *Maxwell-Boltzmann distribution*. Figure 5-1 shows plots of the probability of finding an H_2 molecule with speed u, as a function of u, at three different temperatures. The maximum of the distribution curve corresponds to the *most probable speed*, u_{mp}. The average speed, u_{avg}, is slightly larger than u_{mp}. The *root-mean-square speed*, u_{rms}—the square root of $(u^2)_{average}$—is slightly larger than u_{avg}. These measures of molecular speed are given by:

$$u_{mp} = \sqrt{\frac{2RT}{M}} \qquad u_{avg} = \sqrt{\frac{8RT}{\pi M}} \qquad u_{rms} = \sqrt{\frac{3RT}{M}}$$

(5-9)

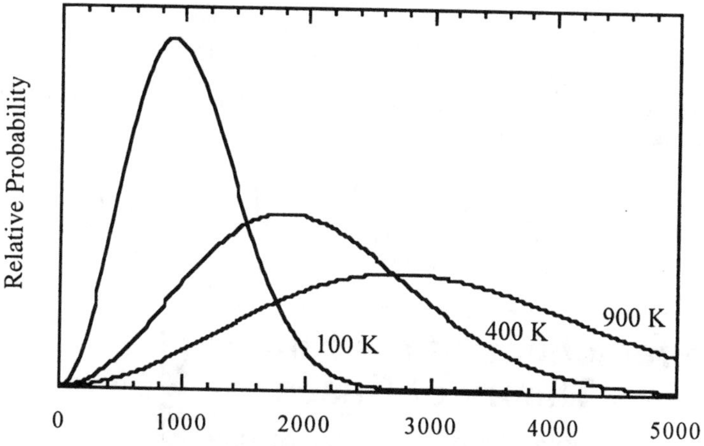

where M is the molar mass in kg/mol.

Figure 5-1. Maxwell-Boltzmann distribution of speeds for H_2 at 100, 400, and 900 K. Note that u_{mp} increases linearly with $T^{1/2}$.

(c) The frequency of collisions per unit area of container wall is:

$$Z = \frac{N_A P}{\sqrt{2\pi MRT}}$$

(5-10)

The rate at which a gas *effuses* (flows out) through a small hole in the container into a vacuum is exactly the rate at which the molecules would collide with a wall area equal to the area of the hole. From Eq. (5-10), the effusion rates of two gases, both at the same pressure and temperature, are in the ratio

$$\frac{Z_1}{Z_2} = \sqrt{\frac{M_2}{M_1}} \qquad (5\text{-}11)$$

This relation is *Graham's law of effusion*: the ratio of the rates of effusion of two gases, at the same P and T, are inversely proportional to the square roots of their molar masses.

(d) Eq. (5-9)—average velocity is inversely proportional to the square root of molar mass—applies to other transport phenomena such as *diffusion, thermal conduction,* and *nonturbulant flow.*

Example 10. Calculate u_{rms} for H_2 molecules at 100 K.

$$u_{rms} = \sqrt{\frac{3RT}{M}} = \sqrt{\frac{3(8.3145 \text{ J mol}^{-1}\text{K}^{-1})(273 \text{ K})}{(2.016 \text{ g/mol})(1 \text{ kg}/1000 \text{ g})}}$$

$$= 1.84 \times 10^3 \text{ (J/kg)}^{1/2} = 1.84 \times 10^3 \left(\frac{\text{kg m}^2\text{s}^{-2}}{\text{kg}}\right)^{1/2} = 1.84 \times 10^3 \text{ m/s}$$

Example 11. Compute the relative rates of effusion of H_2 and CO_2 through a fine pinhole.

$$\frac{\text{rate }(H_2)}{\text{rate }(CO_2)} = \sqrt{\frac{M(CO_2)}{M(H_2)}} = \sqrt{\frac{44.0}{2.016}} = 4.67$$

Predictions of the Kinetic Theory of Gases:

- The molar kinetic energy of gas molecules depends only on T: $E = \frac{3}{2} RT$.

- Molecular speed is proportional to $\sqrt{T/M}$.

Problems

5.1 The vapor pressure of water at 25°C is 23.8 torr. Express this in (a) atm, (b) kPa.   *Ans.* (a) 0.0313 atm, (b) 3.17 kPa

5.2 Chlorine gas is evolved at the anode of a commercial electrolysis cell at the rate of 3.65 L/min, at a temperature of 647°C. On its way to the intake pump it is cooled to 63°C. Calculate the rate of intake to the pump assuming the pressure has remained constant.
          Ans. 1.33 L/min

5.3 What is the volume of 1.216 g of $SO_2(g)$ at 18°C and 755 torr?
          Ans. 456 cm^3

5.4 Compute the molar mass of a gas whose density at 40°C and 785 torr is 1.286 kg/m^3.   *Ans.* 32.0 g/mol

5.5 A collapsed balloon and its load weighs 216 kg. To what volume should it be inflated with H_2 gas in order to launch it from a mountain top at –12°C and 628 torr? The density of air under these conditions is 1.11 g/L.   *Ans.* 210 m^3

5.6 A vacuum tube was sealed off at a pressure of 1.2×10^{-5} torr at 27°C. Its volume is 100 cm^3. Compute the number of gas molecules remaining in the tube.   *Ans.* 3.9×10^{13} molecules

5.7 500 cm^3 of a gas at STP weighs 0.581 g. The composition of the gas is 92.24% C, 7.76% H. What is the molecular formula?
          Ans. C_2H_2

5.8 How many grams of O_2 are contained in 10.5 L of oxygen measured over water at 25°C and 740 torr? The vapor pressure of water at 25°C is 24 torr.   *Ans.* 12.9 g

5.9 A spark was passed through a 50 cm^3 sample of a H_2/O_2 mixture in a gas buret at 18°C and 1.00 atm; the formation of water went to completion. The resulting dry gas had a volume of 10 cm^3 at 18°C, 1.00 atm. What was the initial mole fraction of H_2 in the mixture if (a) the residual gas after sparking was H_2, (b) the residual gas was O_2?   *Ans.* $X(H_2) = $ (a) 0.73, (b) 0.53

5.10 Lithium reacts with hydrogen to produce lithium hydride, LiH. Sometimes the product is contaminated with unreacted Li metal. The extent of the contamination can be determined by measuring the amount of H_2 gas generated by reacting a sample with water,

$$LiH + H_2O \rightarrow LiOH + H_2, \quad 2\,Li + 2\,H_2O \rightarrow 2\,LiOH + H_2$$

A 0.205 g sample of contaminated LiH yielded 561 mL of gas measured over water at 22°C and a total pressure of 731 torr. Calculate the percent by weight of Li metal in the sample. The vapor pressure of water at 22°C is 20 torr.   *Ans.* 37%

Chapter 6
THERMOCHEMISTRY

IN THIS CHAPTER:

✔ *Heat, Energy, and Enthalpy*
✔ *Rules of Thermochemistry*
✔ *Heat Associated with a Temperature Change*
✔ *Heat Associated with a Phase Change*
✔ *Heat Associated with a Chemical Reaction*

Heat, Energy, and Enthalpy

Energy can be transferred to (or from) a chemical system from (or to) the surroundings in the form of heat q or work w. The *first law of thermodynamics* states that the change in the system's *internal energy E* is equal to the sum of the heat and work inputs (or outputs):

$$\Delta E = q + w \qquad (6\text{-}1)$$

where $\Delta E = E_{final} - E_{initial}$. The first law of thermodynamics can be thought of as an extension of the mechanical law of conservation of energy to include heat. Notice that positive heat or work increases the energy of the system, negative heat or work decreases the energy. The

42

internal energy change includes changes in the energies of atomic and molecular motion, changes in the energies of atomic and molecular interactions, and changes associated with a chemical reaction.

Heat energy flows to or from the surroundings when there is a difference in temperature, when a chemical reaction or change of state takes place, or when work is done on or by the system. Unlike P, V, T, and E, heat is not a function of the state of the system. We cannot speak of a system "having heat"; q refers only to energy in transit.

Work is done on (or by) a chemical system when the system is compressed (or is expanded). Thus when V is constant, $w = 0$ and

$$\Delta E = q_V \tag{6-2}$$

where the subscript reminds us that V is constant.

When the pressure is constant, $w = -P\,\Delta V$, $q = \Delta E - w$, or $q_P = \Delta E + P\,\Delta V$. Since E, P, and V are all variables associated with the state of the system, we can define a state function called the *enthalpy*,

$$H = E + PV \tag{6-3}$$

and, for a process occurring at *constant pressure*, the change in enthalpy is

$$\Delta H = \Delta E + P\,\Delta V = q_P \tag{6-4}$$

For most chemical processes, we can think of energy and enthalpy as nearly identical since heat transfer is usually much more important than work performed. However, since the work term can be significant, we must maintain the distinction between E and H.

Essential Points

- At constant volume, heat transferred equals the change in internal energy: $q_V = \Delta E$

- At constant pressure, heat transferred equals the change in enthalpy: $q_P = \Delta H$

- Enthalpy is defined by: $H = E + PV$

We will use the joule (J) to measure energy, enthalpy, and heat. Other energy units which may be encountered are listed in Table 6-1.

Table 6-1. Some Common Energy Units

Energy unit	Unit symbol	Definition
joule (SI)	J	$1 J = 1 kg m^2 s^{-1} = 1 Nm$
calorie	cal	$1 cal = 4.184 J$
Calorie*	Cal	$1 Cal = 10^3 cal$
liter-atmosphere	L atm	$1 L atm = 101.325 J$

* the nutritionists' calorie

Rules of Thermochemistry

The internal energy and the enthalpy of a system depend only on the *state* of the system, as specified by parameters such as V, P, and T. When a system goes from an initial to a final state, ΔE and ΔH depend only on those two states, and are independent of the path taken between them. This path-independence implies *two important rules*:

1. ΔE and ΔH for a reverse process are exactly the negatives of the values for the related forward process. For example, it requires 6.02 kJ of heat to melt 1 mole of ice to liquid water at 0°C, 1 atm. This is a constant pressure process and $\Delta H = +6.02$ kJ/mol. Then for the reverse process, freezing liquid water to ice at 0°C, 1 atm, $\Delta H = -6.02$ kJ/mol, i.e., we must transfer 6.02 kJ from 1 mole of liquid water to convert it to ice.

2. If a process can be imagined to occur in successive steps, ΔH for the overall process is equal to the sum of the enthalpy changes for the individual steps. This rule, sometimes called *Hess's law of constant heat summation*, has many applications in thermochemistry.

Heat Associated with a Temperature Change

The *heat capacity* of a body is defined as the amount of heat required to increase the temperature of the body 1 K. The heat capacity itself may depend on temperature, but we will ignore this complication. For the same reasons that we distinguish between internal energy and enthalpy, we distinguish between heat capacity at constant volume, C_V, and heat capacity at constant pressure, C_P. For pure substances, we often use the *molar heat capacity* (heat capacity per mole) or the *specific heat capacity* (heat capacity per gram). This distinction is clear from the units of C: J/K for an entire body, J/mol•K for one mole of a pure substance, J/g•K for one gram of a pure substance.

If a substance of heat capacity C_V J/K is heated or cooled at constant V through a temperature change ΔT, the heat transferred is

$$q_V = \Delta E = C_V \Delta T \tag{6-5}$$

or at constant P,
$$q_P = \Delta H = C_P \Delta T \tag{6-6}$$

Ordinarily E and H are *extensive*, i.e., they are proportional to the amount (extent) of the system. If we use a molar heat capacity or a specific heat capacity, however, the heat transferred and the change in E or H refers to 1 mol or 1 g of the substance, and we must multiply by n or m to correct ΔE or ΔH to the actual amount of substance.

Example 1. What is the enthalpy change when 100 g of copper is heated from 10°C to 100°C? $C_P(\text{Cu}) = 0.389$ J/g•K.

$$\Delta H = mC_P \Delta T = (100 \text{ g})(0.389 \text{ J/g•K})(90 \text{ K}) = 3.5 \times 10^3 \text{ J}$$

Heat Added to Change Temperature:

- at constant volume: $q_V = \Delta E = C_V \Delta T$
- at constant pressure: $q_P = \Delta H = C_P \Delta T$

Heat Associated with a Phase Change

The heat required to melt a substance is called the *heat of fusion*, or since such processes are normally carried out at constant pressure, the *enthalpy of fusion*, $q_{fus} = \Delta H_{fus}$. Similarly, the heat required for vaporization is the *heat (enthalpy) of vaporization*, $q_{vap} = \Delta H_{vap}$. The heat required to convert a solid directly to the gaseous state is the *heat (enthalpy) of sublimation*, $q_{sub} = \Delta H_{sub}$.

Remember!

Heat Needed to Change
Phase at Constant Pressure:

- Fusion (solid → liquid): $q_{fus} = \Delta H_{fus}$
- Vaporization (liquid → gas): $q_{vap} = \Delta H_{vap}$
- Sublimation (solid → gas): $q_{sub} = \Delta H_{sub}$

Example 2. How much heat is required to convert 40 g of ice at −10°C to steam at 120°C? The specific heat capacities of ice, liquid water, and steam are, respectively, 2.1, 4.2, and 2.0 J/g·K; q_{fus}(ice) = 6.02 kJ/mol and q_{vap}(water) = 40.7 kJ/mol.

The process can be divided into five steps:
Heating ice from −10 to 0°C:
$$(1) \quad q = (40 \text{ g})(2.1 \text{ J/g·K})(10 \text{ K}) = 0.84 \times 10^3 \text{ J}$$
Melting ice at 0°C:
$$(2) \quad q = (6.02 \text{ kJ/mol})(40 \text{ g})/(18.02 \text{ g/mol}) = 13.4 \text{ kJ}$$
Heating water from 0 to 100°C:
$$(3) \quad q = (40 \text{ g})(4.2 \text{ J/g·K})(100 \text{ K}) = 16.8 \times 10^3 \text{ J}$$
Vaporizing water at 100°C:
$$(4) \quad q = (40.7 \text{ kJ/mol})(40 \text{ g})/(18.02 \text{ g/mol}) = 90.3 \text{ kJ}$$
Heating steam from 100 to 120°C:
$$(5) \quad q = (40 \text{ g})(2.0 \text{ J/g·K})(20 \text{ K}) = 1.6 \times 10^3 \text{ J}$$
Applying Rule 2, the total heat required is the sum of steps 1 - 5:
$$q_{total} = 0.84 + 13.4 + 16.8 + 90.3 + 1.6 = 122.9 \text{ kJ}$$

Heat Associated with a Chemical Reaction

We usually will be concerned with reactions at constant pressure so that $q_{rxn} = \Delta H_{rxn}$. Unless otherwise stated, ΔH for a chemical reaction refers to the enthalpy change when the moles of reactant and product species are equal to their coefficients in the balanced equation,

e.g., $2 CO(g) + O_2(g) \rightarrow 2 CO_2(g)$ $\Delta H° = -565.98$ kJ

Standard States. The superscript "o" or degree sign on ΔH designates a *standard enthalpy change*, that is, an enthalpy change when the reactants start out in standard states and the products end up in standard states. *Standard states* are defined as follows:

1. For a solid, liquid, gas or the solvent in a solution: The pure material at 1 atm pressure and 25°C.
2. For a solute in a solution: The ideal 1 molar solution (1 mol solute per liter of solution) at 1 atm and 25°C.

The 1-atm pressure specification is usually not very important for liquids and solids, but is vital for gases. Some books define the standard pressure as 1 bar. Fortunately ΔH is not strongly dependent on pressure, and since 1 bar is very close to 1 atm, numerical values of $\Delta H°$ show only small differences which usually can be overlooked.

Exothermic and Endothermic Reactions. The sign of ΔH tells us whether heat is released (negative ΔH) or absorbed (positive ΔH). We say that a reaction which releases heat is *exothermic* and one which absorbs heat is *endothermic*. Thus in the above reaction, 565.98 kJ is *released* when 2 mol of gaseous CO_2 at 1 atm, 25°C, is formed in the exothermic reaction of 2 mol of CO (g) and 1 mol of $O_2(g)$, both at 1 atm, 25°C.

Enthalpies of Formation. The following reaction describes the formation of a compound from the constituent elements in their most stable forms at 1 atm, 25°C, the *standard reference states*.

$$\tfrac{1}{2} H_2(g) + \tfrac{1}{2} I_2(s) \rightarrow HI(g) \qquad \Delta H_f° = +26.48 \text{ kJ/mol}$$

The subscript "f" on $\Delta H°$ reminds us that this is a formation reaction. In a formation reaction, we are specifically concerned with the product and so write the reaction so that the product has unit stoichiometric coefficient even though we often encounter fractional coefficients for reactants; $\Delta H_f°$ values have units of kJ/mol to emphasize this point.

Table 6-2 lists some values of $\Delta H_f°$ at 25°C. Note the absence of entries for $H_2(g)$, $I_2(s)$, and C(graphite), and all other elements in their standard reference states. By definition $\Delta H_f° = 0$ for all elements in their most stable states. By a special convention, $\Delta H_f° = 0$ for $H^+(aq)$.

A table of standard enthalpies of formation can be used, following rule 2 above, to compute the enthalpy change for any reaction involving species for which values of $\Delta H_f°$ can be found.

Example 3. Compute the standard enthalpy change for the reaction

$$PCl_5(g) + H_2O(g) \rightarrow POCl_3(g) + 2 HCl(g)$$

Table 6-2. Standard Enthalpies of Formation at 25°C (kJ/mol)

Substance	ΔH_f°	Substance	ΔH_f°	Substance	ΔH_f°
$Al_2O_3(s)$	−1675.7	$FeS(s)$	−100.0	$NO_2(g)$	33.18
$Br_2(g)$	30.91	$Fe_2O_3(s)$	−824.2	$N_2O_4(g)$	9.16
$Br(g)$	111.88	$H(g)$	218.0	$O(g)$	249.17
$C(diam.)$	1.90	$H_2O(g)$	−241.81	$O_3(g)$	142.7
$CO(g)$	−110.52	$H_2O(l)$	−285.83	$OH^-(aq)$	−229.99
$CO_2(g)$	−393.51	$HBr(g)$	−36.40	$PCl_3(l)$	−319.7
$CaO(s)$	−635.1	$HCl(g)$	−92.31	$PCl_3(g)$	−287.0
$CaCO_3(s)$	−1207.1	$H_2S(g)$	−20.63	$PCl_5(g)$	−374.9
$CaC_2(s)$	−59.8	$I_2(g)$	62.44	$POCl_3(g)$	−558.5
$Cl^-(aq)$	−167.16	$N(g)$	472.70	$SO_2(g)$	−296.83
$Fe^{2+}(aq)$	−89.1	$NO(g)$	90.25	$SO_3(g)$	−395.72

We can imagine carrying out this reaction by first dissociating the reactant molecules to their constituent elements and then recombining the elements to form the products:

$$PCl_5(g) \rightarrow P(s) + 2\tfrac{1}{2}\, Cl_2(g) \qquad \Delta H^\circ = -\Delta H_f^\circ = +374.9 \text{ kJ}$$

$$H_2O(g) \rightarrow H_2(g) + \tfrac{1}{2}\, O_2(g) \qquad \Delta H^\circ = -\Delta H_f^\circ = +241.8 \text{ kJ}$$

$$P(s) + \tfrac{1}{2}\, O_2(g) + 1\tfrac{1}{2}\, Cl_2(g) \rightarrow POCl_3(g) \qquad \Delta H^\circ = \Delta H_f^\circ = -558.5 \text{ kJ}$$

$$H_2(g) + Cl_2(g) \rightarrow 2\, HCl(g) \qquad \Delta H^\circ = 2\, \Delta H_f^\circ = -184.6 \text{ kJ}$$

Adding the four equations and the ΔH's, we have

$$PCl_5(g) + H_2O(g) \rightarrow POCl_3(g) + 2\, HCl(g) \qquad \Delta H^\circ = -126.4 \text{ kJ}$$

We can generalize the procedure used in Example 3 as follows:

> The enthalpy change of any reaction is equal to the sum of the enthalpies of formation of the products minus the sum of the enthalpies of formation of the reactants, each ΔH_f° multiplied by the stoichiometric coefficient of the substance in the balanced equation.

This can be expressed by the equation (p = products, r = reactants):

$$\Delta H^{o} = \sum_{p} n_{p}\, \Delta H_{f,p}^{\,o} - \sum_{r} n_{r}\, \Delta H_{f,r}^{\,o}$$

(6-7)

The calculation of ΔH° from enthalpies of formation applies, strictly speaking, only to the reaction of reactants in standard states to form products in standard states. Nonetheless, calculations of ΔH° are *very useful* in the general case because ΔH is usually not very sensitive to conditions so that ΔH° provides us with a good semi-quantitative estimate of the reaction energy in most situations.

Problems

6.1 (a) How many joules are required to heat 100 g of iron ($C = 0.45$ J/g•K) from 10°C to 100°C? (b) The same quantity of heat as in (a) is added to 100 g of aluminum ($C = 0.91$ J/g•K) at 10°C. What is the final temperature? *Ans.* (a) 4.0 kJ, (b) 54°C

6.2 How much heat is given up when 20.0 g of steam at 100°C is condensed and cooled to 20°C? $\Delta H_{vap} = 40.7$ kJ/mol, $C_{p} = 75.4$ J/mol·K *Ans. a = –51.9 kJ*

6.3 What is the heat of sublimation of $I_2(s)$? *Ans.* 62.44 kJ/mol

6.4 The enthalpy of combustion of acetylene gas, $C_2H_2(g)$, at 25°C is –1299.58 kJ/mol. Determine the enthalpy of formation of acetylene. *Ans.* $\Delta H_f^{\circ} = +226.73$ kJ/mol

6.5 Compute ΔH° for the reaction

$$CaC_2(s) + 2\,H_2O(l) \rightarrow C_2H_2(g) + Ca(OH)_2(s)$$

$\Delta H_f^{\circ} = -986.1$ kJ/mol for $Ca(OH)_2(s)$. *Ans.* – 127.9 kJ

6.6 Compute ΔH° for the thermite reaction

$$2\,Al(s) + Fe_2O_3(s) \rightarrow 2\,Fe(s) + Al_2O_3(s)$$ *Ans.* –851.5 kJ

6.7 Compute ΔH° for the hypothetical upper-atmosphere reaction

$$N(g) + O(g) \rightarrow NO(g)$$ *Ans.* –631.6 kJ

6.8 Compute ΔH° for the reaction

$$FeS(s) + 2\,H^{+}(aq) \rightarrow Fe^{2+}(aq) + H_2S(g)$$ *Ans.* –9.7 kJ

6.9 What is the heat of solution of HCl(g) in water? *Hint*: HCl is completely ionized in dilute solutions to $H^{+}(aq)$ and $Cl^{-}(aq)$.

Ans. –74.85 kJ/mol

6.10 The heats of combustion, forming $CO_2(g)$ and $H_2O(l)$, of ethane, $C_2H_6(g)$, and ethylene, $C_2H_4(g)$, are –1559.8 and –1410.9 kJ/mol, respectively. Compute ΔH for the reaction

$$C_2H_4(g) + H_2(g) \rightarrow C_2H_6(g)$$ *Ans.* –136.9 kJ

Chapter 7
ATOMIC STRUCTURE

IN THIS CHAPTER:

✔ *Historical Background*
✔ *Quantum Mechanics and the Hydrogen Atom*
✔ *The Pauli Principle and the Periodic Table*

Historical Background

Several key discoveries in the late 19th and early 20th centuries led to our understanding of the structure of atoms.

(1) In 1885, J. J. Balmer found that an electric discharge through H_2 produces excited H atoms which emit light at discrete frequencies, ν, expressed by the empirical Rydberg equation,

$$\nu = R\left(\frac{1}{n_1^2} - \frac{1}{n_2^2}\right)$$

(7-1)

where $R = 3.29 \times 10^{15}$ s^{-1} and n_1, n_2 are integers, $n_2 > n_1 \geq 1$.

(2) In 1888, it was found that when light strikes a metal electrode in a vacuum tube, electrons are ejected from the metal in the *photoelectric effect*. For frequencies less than a cutoff frequency ν_0, no electrons are ejected, but above that frequency, electrons are ejected with kinetic energies proportional to $(\nu - \nu_0)$.

(3) In 1911, Ernest Rutherford showed that α-particles (we now know that α-particles are helium nuclei) are sometimes scattered through large angles when they strike gold atoms, a result which could be understood only in terms of a very small atomic nucleus containing most of the mass of the atom.

According to classical theory, light is wavelike with frequency v (measured in hertz, 1 Hz = 1 s^{-1}) and wavelength λ, which are related by $\lambda v = c$, where c is the speed of light, 2.998×10^8 m/s. Beginning in 1900 with the work of Max Planck, it became apparent that light can also behave like a particle. The "particle of light" is called a *photon*, and each photon carries an energy, $E = hv$, where h is Planck's constant, 6.626×10^{-34} J•s. In 1905, Albert Einstein explained the photoelectric effect in terms of photons: When a photon strikes the metal, an electron may be ejected if the photon carries energy greater than the binding energy of the electron in the metal, $E_{binding} = hv_0$. The electron carries off the excess energy, $h(v - v_0)$, and it was found that the empirical proportionality constant is indeed equal to h. Since light emitted by an excited H atom comes in discrete frequencies, the implication is that the electron must be limited to discrete energy levels and that a transition from a higher level to a lower level is responsible for emission of a photon.

In 1913, Neils Bohr developed a theory for the hydrogen atom which postulated a planetary orbit for the electron about the nucleus. The various allowed energy levels corresponded to different orbit radii. Bohr was able to calculate the Rydberg constant R from the mass and charge of the electron, and the theory appeared to be a great success. Unfortunately, however, it proved impossible to extend Bohr's theory to heavier atoms or to molecules, and it was eventually abandoned in favor of the quantum mechanical description developed by Erwin Schrödinger and Werner Heisenberg in the mid-1920s.

Quantum Mechanics and the Hydrogen Atom

Quantum mechanics began with a daring hypothesis by Louis de Broglie (he was a student at the time): if light has a dualistic wave/particle nature, why not matter? His reasoning led to the prediction that a particle of mass m and velocity υ would exhibit wavelike properties with wavelength

$$\lambda = h/m\upsilon \qquad (7\text{-}2)$$

Thus for an electron beam with $\upsilon = 1.46 \times 10^6$ m/s, Eq. (7-2) gives $\lambda = 5.0$ Å, comparable to the ionic spacing in a crystal. In 1920, it was found that a crystal would indeed diffract an electron beam, and de Broglie's crazy idea was proven!

Once it was established that electrons could behave like waves, physicists began looking for ways of dealing with electrons using their wavelike properties, and in 1926, Schrödinger found the solution. Schrödinger's *wave equation* does not attempt to calculate the trajectory of an electron nor does it make any assumptions about planetary orbits of electrons about nuclei. Rather it computes a *wave function*, the square of which is the *probability density* of finding an electron at some point in space. When applied to the hydrogen atom, the results are similar to those of Bohr, with the following equation for the allowed energies:

$$E_n = -\frac{\mu e^4 Z^2}{8\varepsilon_0^2 h^2 n^2}$$

$$(7\text{-}3)$$

where μ is the reduced mass, $\mu = m_e m_n/(m_e + m_n) \approx m_e$ (m_e and m_n are the masses of the electron and the nucleus), e is the electronic charge, Z is the nuclear charge in units of $|e|$ ($Z = 1$ for H, 2 for He^+), $\varepsilon_0 = 8.854 \times 10^{-12}$ $C^2J^{-1}m^{-1}$ is the permittivity of free space, h is Planck's constant, and n is a positive integer. The energy of the photon emitted from an excited H atom is the difference between allowed energies:

$$E_{n_2} - E_{n_1} = h\nu = \frac{\mu e^4 Z^2}{8\varepsilon_0^2 h^2} \left(\frac{1}{n_1^2} - \frac{1}{n_2^2} \right)$$

$$(7\text{-}4)$$

in agreement with Eq. (7-1).

The integer n in Eq. (7-3), called the *principal quantum number*, determines the energy levels in a one-electron atom or ion and largely determines the average distance of the electron from the nucleus. A complete description of the H atom requires two additional quantum numbers:

The *angular momentum quantum number*, l, defines the shape of the electronic distribution, called an *orbital*. l may have any integral value between 0 and $n - 1$. Chemists often use a letter to represent the numerical value of l:

$l =$	0	1	2	3	4
letter:	s	p	d	f	g

The *magnetic quantum number*, m, describes the orientation of orbitals in space. m may have any integral value between $-l$ and $+l$.

Thus for $l = 0$, $m = 0$, for $l = 1$, $m = \pm1$, 0; in general there are $2l + 1$ values of m.

Essential Point

The quantum numbers (qn) of the H atom:

- The principal qn, $n = 1, 2, 3, \ldots$
- The angular momentum qn, $l = 0, 1, \ldots n - 1$
- The magnetic qn, $m = 0, \pm1, \ldots \pm l$

The shapes of the s, p, and d orbitals are shown in Figure 7-1.

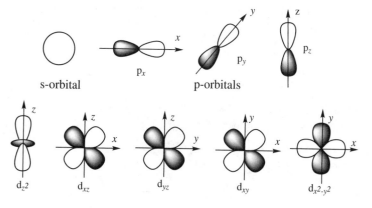

Figure 7-1. Shapes of s, p, and d-orbitals.

Each p-orbital is oriented along one of the cartesian axes with a nodal plane of zero probability perpendicular to that axis. Four of the five d-orbitals have the same shapes with lobes along the x and y axes $(d_{x^2-y^2})$, between the x and y axes (d_{xy}), between the y and z axes (d_{yz}), or between the x and z axes (d_{xz}). In each case, there are two nodal planes. The d_{z^2}-orbital has lobes along the z-axis and a "doughnut"-shaped ring in the xy-plane; two conical nodes separate the lobes from the doughnut. The different shading of the lobes of the p- and d-orbitals represent the $+$ and $-$ signs of the wave functions (the signs disappear when the function is squared to get the probability distributions).

The most probable radius for a 1s electron is $r = a_0$, for a 2p electron, $r = 4a_0$, and for a 3d electron, $r = 9a_0$. Thus with increasing n, the electron is, on the average, further from the nucleus.

The Pauli Principle and the Periodic Table

The Schrödinger equation cannot be solved exactly for polyelectronic atoms, but the hydrogen atom provides a good model on which to build an understanding of heavier atoms. The description of atomic structure in terms of orbitals is still valid and the quantum numbers n, l, and m are still useful. For H the energy depends only on n, but orbital energies for heavier atoms depend also on l (but not on m). For a given value of n, orbital energies increase with l, but the 3d and 4s energies are comparable, 4s usually being filled first; similarly 4d and 5s are close in energy with 5s usually filled first.

> The Pauli Principle: No two electrons in an atom can have the same set of all four quantum numbers, n, l, m, and m_s.

For atoms with more than one electron, we must take account of a fourth quantum number, m_s, the *electron spin quantum number*, which has only two values, $m_s = \pm 1/2$. An electron has a magnetic moment which can be rationalized by imagining that electrons spin about an internal axis. Since the spin can be "clockwise" or "counterclockwise", the electron's magnetic moment has two possible orientations described by the quantum number m_s. We must take account of m_s because of the *Pauli principle*, which states that every electron must have a unique set of quantum numbers, n, l, m, and m_s. Thus any orbital characterized by the quantum numbers n, l, and m can accommodate at most two electrons, one with $m_s = +1/2$, the other $-1/2$.

Electronic Configurations. The ground state (the state of lowest energy) of H has a single electron is a 1s orbital, and we use the notation $1s^1$ to describe the electronic configuration. With 2 electrons, He has the ground state configuration $1s^2$. When we come to Li with 3 electrons, we must populate the 2s orbital and the ground state configuration is $1s^2 2s^1$. Table 7-1 shows the ground state configurations for the first 30 elements. In the table, we have used the notation [He], [Ne], and [Ar] to represent the configurations of He, Ne, and Ar; e.g., [Ne] represents the configuration $1s^2 2s^2 2p^6$. This notation focuses our attention on the outermost electrons, the so-called *valence electrons*, which are important in chemical bonding.

The Periodic Table. When Dimitri Mendeleev constructed the periodic table in 1869, he knew nothing of electronic configurations or even of atomic numbers. He grouped elements in order of increasing atomic mass (with a few exceptions, e.g., Ni and Co) arranged in columns of elements with similar chemical properties. We now see that this similarity is due to similar electronic configurations. Thus all alkali metals (Group I) have the valence electron configuration ns^1, all alkaline earth metals (Group II) have the configuration ns^2, all halogens (Group VII) all $ns^2 np^5$, etc.

Atom	Configuration	Atom	Configuration	Atom	Configuration
H	$1s^1$	Na	[Ne] $3s^1$	Sc	[Ar] $4s^2 3d^1$
He	$1s^2$	Mg	[Ne] $3s^2$	Ti	[Ar] $4s^2 3d^2$
Li	[He] $2s^1$	Al	[Ne] $3s^2 3p^1$	V	[Ar] $4s^2 3d^3$
Be	[He] $2s^2$	Si	[Ne] $3s^2 3p^2$	Cr	[Ar] $4s^1 3d^5$
B	[He] $2s^2 2p^1$	P	[Ne] $3s^2 3p^3$	Mn	[Ar] $4s^2 3d^5$
C	[He] $2s^2 2p^2$	S	[Ne] $3s^2 3p^4$	Fe	[Ar] $4s^2 3d^6$
N	[He] $2s^2 2p^3$	Cl	[Ne] $3s^2 3p^5$	Co	[Ar] $4s^2 3d^7$
O	[He] $2s^2 2p^4$	Ar	[Ne] $3s^2 3p^6$	Ni	[Ar] $4s^2 3d^8$
F	[He] $2s^2 2p^5$	K	[Ar] $4s^1$	Cu	[Ar] $4s^1 3d^{10}$
Ne	[He] $2s^2 2p^6$	Ca	[Ar] $4s^2$	Zn	[Ar] $4s^2 3d^{10}$

Table 7-1. Electronic Configurations of Elements 1–30.

Paramagnetism. When electrons pair, their magnetic moments cancel, but atoms (or molecules) with unpaired electrons are *paramagnetic*, i.e., they are attracted by a magnetic field.

Atomic Radii. The electron cloud around an atomic nucleus makes the concept of atomic size somewhat imprecise, but it is useful to refer to an atomic radius. One can arbitrarily divide the distance between centers of two bonded atoms to arrive at two radii, based on the crude picture that two bonded atoms are spheres in contact. If the bonding is covalent, the radius is called a *covalent radius* (see Table 8-2); if it is ionic, the radius is an *ionic radius* (see Table 9-2). The radius for non-bonded atoms may be defined in terms of the distance of closest non-bonding approach; such a measure is called the *van der Waals radius*. These three concepts of size are illustrated in Figure 7-2.

Generalizations regarding atomic size: (1) Within a column of the periodic table, radii increase with increasing atomic number, a result of the increasing value of n for the valence electrons. (2) Within a given period (row) of the table, covalent radii generally decrease with increasing Z; n is constant across the period, but the nuclear charge increases. (3) A cation radius is small compared with the covalent radius of the neutral atom since one or more valence electrons has been removed. (4) An anion radius is significantly greater than the covalent radius of the neutral atom since the extra electron(s) are held less tightly (more electrons, but the same nuclear charge).

Ionization Energy. The energy required to remove an electron from an atom is called the ionization energy (IE). The zero of energy

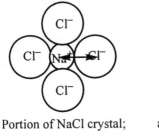

Portion of NaCl crystal;
arrow shows sum of
ionic radii

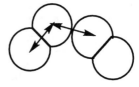

Two Cl_2 molecules in contact;
arrows show twice the covalent
radius and twice the
van der Waals radius.

Figure 7-2. Illustrations of ionic, covalent, and van der Waals radii.

for H is ionization so that IE $= -E_1 = 13.60$ eV. (One electron-volt is the energy acquired by an electron on acceleration through an electric potential difference of 1 V, 1 eV $= 1.6022 \times 10^{-19}$ J.) First ionization energies (IE_1) for other atoms are given in Table 7-2. In general, IE_1 decreases as we descend a column in the periodic table and increases as we move from left to right across the table. Table 7-2 also lists second ionization energies (IE_2), the energy required to remove a second electron. IE_2 is always greater than IE_1, and the difference is greatest when the second electron comes from a different shell than the first, e.g., the alkali metals of Group I.

Although the transition metals (Sc–Cu, for example) appear to fill the 4s orbital before the 3d orbitals, the 4s electrons are the first to be ionized; thus the electronic configuration of Cr^{2+} is [Ar] $3d^4$, and that of Zn^{2+} is [Ar] $3d^{10}$.

Electron Affinity. Most gas-phase atoms can capture an electron to form a gas-phase anion, e.g., $Cl(g) + e^- \rightarrow Cl^-$, $\Delta E = -3.61$ eV. The electron affinity (EA) of Cl is taken to be +3.61 eV. Electron affinities for some other atoms are given in Table 7-2. In general, atoms with nearly completed p-shells have the highest electron affinities; those with completed s- or p-outer shells have negative electron affinities, i.e., they do not accept an extra electron.

Electronegativity. Closely related to ionization energy and electron affinity is the concept of electronegativity, a measure of the ability of an atom to attract shared electrons in a bond. We usually use electronegativities in a qualitative way, for example, to predict bond polarities (see Chapter 8). Electronegativities, on a dimensionless scale ranging from 0 to 4, are given in Table 7-2.

	H							He
IE	13.60							24.58
EA	0.76							<0
EN	2.20							—
	Li	Be	B	C	N	O	F	Ne
IE_1	5.39	9.32	8.30	11.26	14.53	13.62	17.42	21.57
IE_2	75.63	18.21	25.15	24.39	29.60	35.11	34.97	40.96
EA	0.62	<0	0.28	1.26	0.0	1.46	3.40	<0
EN	0.97	1.47	2.01	2.50	3.07	3.50	4.10	—
	Na	Mg	Al	Si	P	S	Cl	Ar
IE_1	5014	7.65	5.99	8.15	10.49	10.36	12.97	15.76
IE_2	47.28	15.04	18.83	16.34	19.72	23.33	23.81	27.63
EA	0.55	<0	0.46	1.39	0.75	2.07	3.62	<0
EN	1.01	1.23	1.47	1.74	2.06	2.44	3.83	—

Table 7-2. Ionization Energies (eV),
Electron Affinities (eV), and Electronegativities

Problems

7.1 When a photon of wavelength $\lambda = 400$ nm strikes a Cs target, an electron is ejected. Calculate the kinetic energy of the electron if the maximum wavelength to obtain a photoelectron from Cs is 660 nm. *Ans.* 1.22 eV

7.2 It has been found that $I_2(g)$ molecules are dissociated into atoms on absorption of light with $\lambda \leq 499.5$ nm. If one photon carries enough energy to dissociate I_2, compute the dissociation energy in kJ/mol. *Ans.* 239.5 kJ/mol

7.3 (a) What is the frequency of light emitted when a He^+ ion undergoes a $n = 2$ to $n = 1$ transition? (b) What is the second ionization energy of He? *Ans.* (a) 9.9×10^{15} s^{-1}, (b) 54.4 eV

7.4 Given the ionization energy of Li and the electron affinity of Cl (Table 7-2), compute ΔE for the reaction

$$Li(g) + Cl(g) \rightarrow Li^+(g) + Cl^-(g) \qquad Ans. \ +172 \text{ kJ/mol}$$

7.5 In a measurement of the quantum efficiency of photosynthesis in green plants, it was found that 8 quanta of red light at 685nm were needed to evolve one molecule of O_2. The average energy storage in the photosynthetic process is 469 kJ per mole of O_2 evolved. What is the energy conversion efficiency in this experiment? *Ans.* 33.5%

7.6 The prominent yellow line in the spectrum of a sodium vapor lamp has a wavelength of 590 nm. What minimum accelerating potential is needed to excite this line in an electron tube containing sodium vapor? *Ans.* 2.10 V

7.7 The iconic radii of S^{2-} and Te^{2-} are 1.84 and 2.21 Å, respectively. What would you predict for the iconic radius of Se^{2-} and for P^{3-} ?

> *Ans.* Since Se falls in between S and Te, one expects an intermediate value; observed value is 1.98 Å. Since P is just to the left of S, a slightly larger value is expected; observed value is 2.12 Å.

7.8 Van der Waals radii for S and Cl are 1.85 and 1.80 Å, repectively. What would you predict for the van der Waals radius of Ar?

> *Ans.* Moving toward the right in the same period the trend continues toward smaller size. The observed value is 1.54 Å

Chapter 8
CHEMICAL BONDING
AND MOLECULAR
STRUCTURE

IN THIS CHAPTER:

✔ Covalent Bonds
✔ Molecular Orbitals
✔ Shapes of Molecules
✔ Isomerism

Introduction

Chemical compounds are of two basic types—ionic and covalent. Ionic compounds such as NH_4Cl and Li_2SO_4 are made up of discrete ions—NH_4^+ and Cl^-, Li^+ and SO_4^{2-}—held together in crystals by electrostatic forces. The structures of ionic crystals will be discussed in Chapter 9. In this chapter, we consider the much larger group of compounds consisting of molecules and polyatomic ions such as CH_4 and H_2O, NH_4^+, and SO_4^{2-}. In these species the atoms are connected by covalent bonds in which the atoms share electrons.

Covalent Bonds

Lewis electron-dot structures. The first great advance in qualitative understanding of chemical bonding was G. N. Lewis's suggestion in 1916 that atoms in stable molecules or ions tend to attain the configuration of the nearest noble gas. For elements on the right side of the periodic table, this means acquiring eight valence electrons, the *octet rule*. Thus when Na and Cl atoms react to form NaCl, Na loses an electron to attain the Ne configuration and Cl gains an electron to attain the Ar configuration:

$$:\overset{..}{\underset{..}{Cl}}\cdot \; + \; Na\cdot \longrightarrow \; :\overset{..}{\underset{..}{Cl}}:^- \; + \; Na^+$$

$$(8\text{-}1)$$

When a covalent bond is formed, the atoms share an electron pair, often obeying the octet rule by sharing electron pairs. For example, C achieves an octet in CH_4 by sharing each of its 4 valence electrons with a H atom, which contributes 1 electron. Similarly N, with 5 valence electrons, achieves an octet in NH_3 by sharing 3 electrons with H atoms, leaving an unshared pair; O, with 6 valence electrons, achieves an octet in H_2O by sharing 2 electrons with H atoms, leaving two unshared pairs. These structures are shown in Figure 8-1, where the shared electron pair is represented by a line between the bonded atoms. Polyatomic ions like NH_4^+ and OH^- also have structures obeying the octet rule. Notice that in the structures of Figure 8-1, H has a share of two electrons, which is as expected if it is to attain the He configuration; we might say that H obeys the *doublet rule*. Similar reasoning applied to covalently bonded transition metals allows an expansion beyond eight electrons.

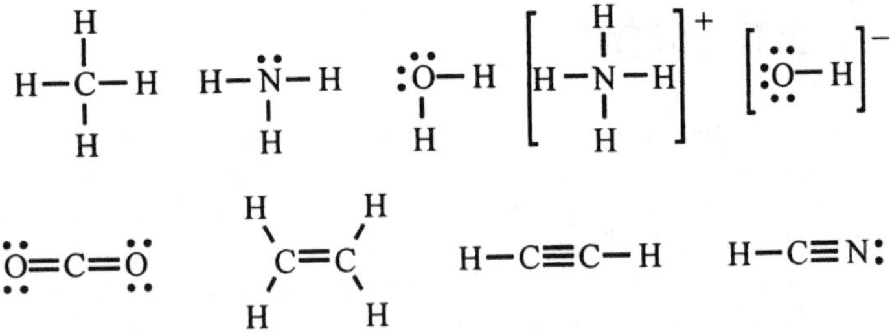

Figure 8-1. Lewis electron-dot structures.

Multiple Bonds. The C and O atoms in molecules like CO_2 and H_2CCH_2 can be understood to obey the octet rule if we assume that two electron pairs are shared, leading to a *double bond*. Still other molecules like HCCH and HCN require the sharing of three electron pairs, a *triple bond*.

You Need to Know

A covalent bond between two atoms involves sharing of 1, 2, or 3 electron pairs—single, double, or triple bonds.

Resonance Structures. Sometimes more than one satisfactory Lewis structure can be written and there is no reason to select one over another. In such cases a single structural formula is inadequate for a correct representation, and we say that the true structure is a *resonance hybrid* of the several structures. Common examples of species requiring resonance structures are ozone, O_3, carbonate ion, CO_3^{2-}, and benzene, C_6H_6. These structures are shown in Figure 8-2. The number of electron pairs shared by two atoms is sometimes called the *bond order* (BO). Thus a single bond has BO = 1, a double bond has BO = 2. In O_3 and C_6H_6, the apparent O-O and C-C bond orders are 1.5; in CO_3^{2-}, the apparent C-O bond order is 1.33; these numbers are averages over the various resonance structures.

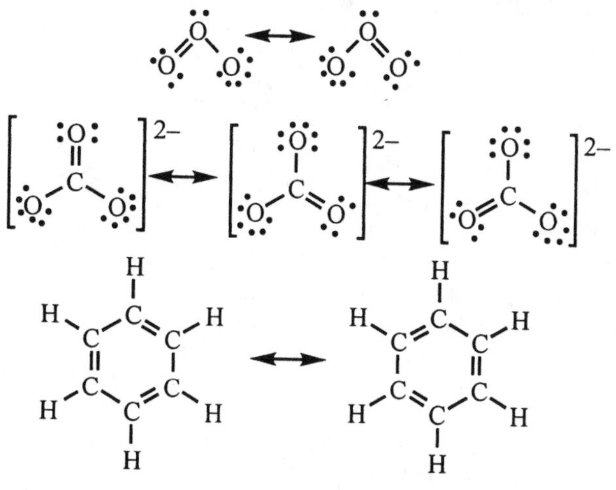

Figure 8-2. Resonance structures.

Formal Charge. Consider an atom in a molecule, e.g., N in NH_3. If we assign half of the electrons shared with H atoms to N and add the two unshared electrons, we have $6/2 + 2 = 5$ electrons assignable to N. Since N contributed 5 valence electrons, we say that the N *formal charge* is zero. Similarly, the other neutral molecules of Figure 8-1 have zero formal charge on each atom. With O_3, however, the central O has 1 unshared pair and half of 3 bonding pairs, $2 + 6/2 = 5$; since O contributed 6 electrons, the formal charge on the central O of O_3 is +1. In each resonance structure, the double-bonded terminal O has 2 unshared pairs and half of 2 bonding pairs, $4 + 4/2 = 6$, so that this O atom is neutral. The singly bonded terminal O atom has 3 unshared pairs and half of a bonding pair, $6 + 2/2 = 7$, so that this O atom has a formal charge of –1. On the average, the terminal O atoms each have formal charges of –1/2. In CO_3^{2-}, the C atom has half of 4 bonding pairs, and thus C is neutral. As in O_3, the doubly bonded O atom is neutral and the singly bonded O atoms have formal charges of –1. On the average each O atom has a formal charge of –2/3. Note that in each case the total charge is the sum of the formal charges.

The Octet Rule

Molecules and ions are most stable when each atom has a share of 8 electrons

- The rule is usually obeyed by C, N, O, and F.

- Exceptions: H shares 2 electrons, Group IA-IIIA elements usually have fewer than 8 electrons, and heavier Group IVA-VIIA elements often have more than 8 electrons.

Exceptions to the Octet Rule. The octet rule is almost always obeyed by the elements in the upper right corner of the periodic table: C, N, O, and F. Although molecules are known that do not satisfy the octet rule, e.g., methyl radical, CH_3, they are unstable, highly reactive, and usually have very short lifetimes.

Molecules with atoms from the left side of the periodic table usually show exceptions to the octet rule. Thus in BF_3, the B has 3 valence electrons, just enough to form 3 electron pair bonds with F. We could formally satisfy the octet rule by invoking 3 resonance structures, each with 1 B=F and 2 B-F bonds, but this would result in a formal charge of -1 on B and, on the average, $+1/3$ on F. Since F is much more electronegative than B, this arrangement seems unlikely and we accept the fact that B does not obey the octet rule.

Atoms from the second row of the periodic table—Si, P, S, and Cl—often form molecules in which one of these atoms has a share of more than 8 electrons, e.g., PCl_5 and SF_6. This kind of exception to the octet rule is usually rationalized by saying that these atoms can use their empty 3d orbitals to assist in bond formation, thus allowing for more than 8 electrons.

Molecular Orbitals

An approximate *molecular orbital* (MO) wave function for H_2 can be constructed by adding H 1s atomic orbitals for atoms A and B,

$$\sigma_{1s} = N\,(1s_A + 1s_B) \tag{8-2}$$

$$(\sigma_{1s})^2 = N^2\,[(1s_A)^2 + (1s_B)^2 + 2\,(1s_A)(1s_B)] \tag{8-3}$$

Figure 8-3 shows the squares of the 1s orbital functions (dashed lines), adjusted so that the amplitudes refer to one electron on each atom, together with the square of the MO wave function, Eq. (8-3), with N adjusted so that the function amplitude refers to the two electrons of H_2, plotted along a line extending through the nuclei . The first two terms, $(1s_A)^2 + (1s_B)^2$, are the same as the original atomic orbitals (AOs), but the third term is new. This crossterm is significantly different from zero only in the region where the two AOs overlap, and we see that the MO function is larger than the sum of the two AO functions in the overlap region and somewhat smaller elsewhere. Thus the electrons are partially localized between the nuclei, a kind of "electrostatic glue" holding the molecule together.

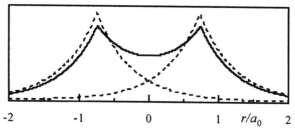

-2   -1   0   1 r/a_0 2

Figure 8-3. Formation of the bonding MO (solid line) for H_2 from two H 1s AOs (dashed lines).

The H_2 molecular orbital function is designated σ_{1s}; the designation σ tells us that the MO has cylindrical symmetry about the bond axis and thus is the molecular analog of an atomic s-orbital (σ is the Greek equivalent of s), and the subscript reminds us that the MO function is constructed from H 1s AO functions.

There is another way of combining two 1s AO functions to form a molecular orbital,

$$\sigma_{1s}{}^* = N\,(1s_A - 1s_B) \tag{8-4}$$

Because of the negative sign, the 1s AO functions cancel in the region of overlap so that there is an absence of electron density between the two nuclei. Thus $\sigma_{1s}{}^*$ is called an *antibonding molecular orbital* and is distinguished from the bonding orbital of Eq. (8-2) by the *. The energy of the σ_{1s}^* orbital is considerably greater than that of the σ_{1s} orbital, so that the ground state of H_2 has two electrons in σ_{1s}, and H_2 is a stable molecule.

If we attempt to make He_2, the third and fourth electrons would have to be placed in the σ_{1s}^* MO. The sum of the squares of the MO's is just the sum of the two AO's, since the cross-terms cancel,

$$\sigma_{1s}{}^2 + \sigma_{1s}{}^{*2} = 1s_A^2 + 1s_B^2$$

Thus with both σ_{1s} and σ_{1s}^* filled, there is no net bonding, and He_2 doesn't exist.

We can also construct σ_{2s} and $\sigma_{2s}{}^*$ MOs which are very similar to $\sigma_{1\sigma}$ and σ_1^*. Construction of MO's from 2p AOs is also possible, but now there are two kinds of overlap, shown in Figure 8-4. If the $2p_z$ orbitals overlap head-to-head along the bond axis, MOs with cylindrical symmetry are formed; if the overlap is between $2p_z$ lobes of the same sign, we get the bonding σ_{2p} orbital, but if the signs are different, we have the antibonding σ_{2p}^* orbital. The $2p_x$ and $2p_y$ orbitals overlap side-by-side to form MOs which are not symmetric

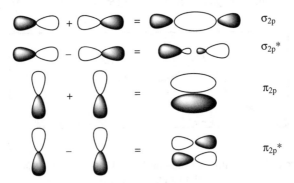

Figure 8-4 Molecular orbitals derived from 2p AOs.

about the bond axis. These MOs have symmetry analogous to that of the 2p AO's, and are called π (bonding) and π^* (anti-bonding) orbitals. A qualitative energy level diagram for the MO's formed from 2s-2s and 2p-2p overlap in a diatomic molecule is shown in Figure 8-5.

Figure 8-5. MO energy-level diagram for diatomic molecules (energy increases vertically). Note that there are two π_{2p} and two π_{2p}^* orbitals, derived from the $2p_x$ and $2p_y$ atomic orbitals.

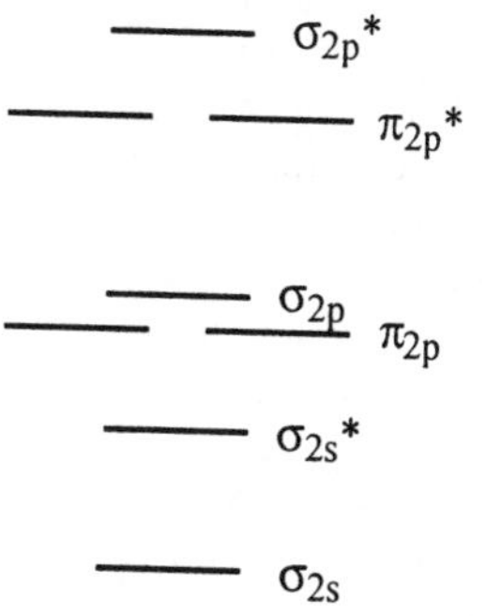

Electronic configurations of the diatomic molecules, Li_2–Ne_2 are given in Table 8-1. The number of net bonding electron pairs (bonding pairs – anti-bonding pairs) is the *bond order*, also given in Table 8-1. Be_2 and Ne_2 are predicted to have BO = 0 and these molecules do not exist. The bond orders for N_2, O_2, and F_2 are consistent with the electron-dot structures, BO = 3 for N_2, 2 for O_2, and 1 for F_2. We cannot write structures obeying the octet rule for Li_2, B_2, and C_2, but these molecules exist and their properties are in accord with MO theory predictions. B_2 and O_2 each has 2 electrons in the pair of π_{2p} or π_{2p}^* MOs; one electron will occupy each MO with parallel spins so that B_2 and O_2 are predicted to be *paramagnetic,* as is observed. This prediction for O_2 is *not* in accord with the electron-dot structure.

Molecule	Electronic Configuration	Bond Order
Li_2	σ_{2s}^2	1
Be_2	$\sigma_{2s}^2\sigma_{2s}^{*2}$	0
B_2	$\sigma_{2s}^2\sigma_{2s}^{*2}\pi_{2p}^2$	1
C_2	$\sigma_{2s}^2\sigma_{2s}^{*2}\pi_{2p}^4$	2
N_2	$\sigma_{2s}^2\sigma_{2s}^{*2}\pi_{2p}^4\sigma_{2p}^2$	3
O_2	$\sigma_{2s}^2\sigma_{2s}^{*2}\pi_{2p}^4\sigma_{2p}^2\pi_{2p}^{*2}$	2
F_2	$\sigma_{2s}^2\sigma_{2s}^{*2}\pi_{2p}^4\sigma_{2p}^2\pi_{2p}^{*4}$	1
Ne_2	$\sigma_{2s}^2\sigma_{2s}^{*2}\pi_{2p}^4\sigma_{2p}^2\pi_{2p}^{*4}\sigma_{2p}^{*2}$	0

Table 8-1. Electronic Configurations and Bond Orders for Li_2–Ne_2.

The description of bonding for *homonuclear* diatomic molecules (molecules containing two identical atoms) is qualitatively correct for *heteronuclear* diatomics (molecules with two different atoms). Thus we can predict that CO, which has 10 valence electrons and is *isoelectronic* with N_2, has a bond order of 3. NO, with 11 valence electrons, has a single electron in the π_{2p}^* orbital and a bond order of 2.5; with an odd number of electrons, NO is paramagnetic.

The qualitative picture of σ and π molecular orbitals can be extended to molecules with three or more atoms. Thus the double bond of ethylene, $H_2C=CH_2$, and the triple bond of acetylene, $HC\equiv CH$, can be understood in terms of a σ-bonding pair and one or two π-bonding pairs of electrons.

Don't Forget

Molecular orbital theory tells us that:

- Molecular orbitals are of two types—σ with cylindrical symmetry about the bond axis, and π with a nodal plane containing the bond axis.

- Every bonding orbital has a higher-energy antibonding counterpart with a nodal plane perpendicular to the bond axis.

Shapes of Molecules

Bond Lengths. The distance between two atoms of the same type is approximately constant from one compound to another if the bond order is the same. The length of a single covalent bond can be estimated by the sum of the covalent radii of the two atoms. A short list of covalent radii is given in Table 8-2.

The lengths of the C-C bonds in $H_3C–CH_3$, $H_2C=CH_2$, and $HC\equiv CH$ are 154, 133, and 120 pm, respectively. For atoms similar in size to C, a double bond is about 21 pm shorter and a triple bond is 34

You Need to Know

Length of single bond = sum of covalent radii, double bonds about 21 pm shorter, triple bonds about 34 pm shorter. Average lengths for resonance structures to get approximate bond length for molecule.

Table 8-2. Single-Bond Covalent Radii (pm)

H	37	C	77	S	104
Li	135	N	117	F	64
Be	90	Si	70	Cl	99
B	80	P	110	Br	114
Al	125	O	66	I	133

Table 8-3. Examples of Bond Length Estimation

Molecule	Bond	Prediction	Obs. Length
CH_3Cl	C–Cl	$77 + 99 = 176$	177 pm
$(CH_3)_2O$	C–O	$77 + 66 = 143$	143 pm
H_2CO	C=O	$77 + 66 - 21 = 122$	122 pm
ICN	C≡N	$77 + 70 - 34 = 113$	116 pm

pm shorter than a single bond between the same atoms. In the case of resonance, a bond length is approximately the average of the values expected for the resonance structures. Some applications of this rule are shown in Table 8-3.

Bond Angles. *Valence-shell electron pair repulsion* (VSEPR) theory gives reasonably accurate predictions of bond angles in a molecule. VSEPR theory uses a simple electrostatic model in which groups of electrons around a central atom repel one another and occupy positions as far apart as possible. The number of electron groups, called the *steric* *number* (SN), is the number of unshared electron pairs plus the number of bonding groups; a bonding group is defined as the 2 electrons of a single bond, the 4 electrons of a double bond, or the 6 electrons of a triple bond. Thus, for example, $HC{\equiv}CH$ has 2 electrons in each C-H bond and 6 electrons in the $C{\equiv}C$ bond, so SN(C) = 2. The two groups of electrons get as far away from each other as possible—on opposite sides of the C atom. VSEPR theory predicts a linear molecule. The other predictions of VSEPR theory are as follows:

Predictions of VSEPR Theory:

- SN = 2, linear molecule, 180° bond angles,
- SN = 3, trigonal planar, 120° bond angles,
- SN = 4, tetrahedral, 109.5° bond angles,
- SN = 5, trigonal bipyramidal, 120 & 90° angles
- SN = 6, octahedral, 90 & 180° bond angles.

The basic molecular shapes are shown in Figure 8-6. Note that the words *tetrahedral* and *octahedral* refer to the four- and eight-sided solids formed by connecting the ligand atoms, not to the coordination numbers, which are 4 and 6, respectively.

Bond angles are sometimes rationalized by invoking atomic *orbital hydbridization*. Thus 180° angles are said to result from sp hybrids, 120° angles from sp^2 hybrids, and 109.5° angles from sp^3 hybrids. This concept of hybrid orbitals is fundamentally flawed, but it has become a part of the language of chemists. You will no doubt hear of hybrid orbitals; take sp, sp^2, and sp^3 as synonyms for 180°, 120°, 109.5°.

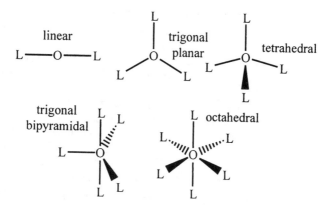

Figure 8-6. The Five VSEPR Molecular Shapes.

If all ligands are the same, the VSEPR bond angle predictions are almost always exact. Thus in CH_4 (SN = 4) and SF_6 (SN = 6), the structures are perfectly tetrahedral and octahedral, respectively. In NH_3 and H_2O, both with SN = 4, $\angle$ H-N-H = 107.3°, $\angle$ H-O-H = 104.5°. This departure from the predicted 109.5° angle is due to the greater repulsion of the lone pairs on N and O. Similarly, the two electron pairs in a double bond are more repulsive than a single bonding pair so that the H-C-H bond angle in $H_2C=CH_2$ is 116.6°, slightly smaller than the 120° angle predicted for SN = 3.

For linear, trigonal planar, tetrahedral, and octahedral structures, all ligand positions are equivalent. The trigonal bipyramidal structure, on the other hand, has two kinds of ligand sites—*axial* and *equatorial*. Each axial electron pair is 90° away from three equatorial pairs and 180° away from the other axial pair. Each equatorial pair is 90° away from two axial pairs and 120° from the other two equatorial pairs. Electron repulsion is slightly greater for the axial pairs, so that a more repulsive electron pair is better off at an equatorial site. Thus for an SN = 5 molecule with an unshared electron pair such as SF_4, the unshared pair will occupy an equatorial site. Highly electronegative ligand atoms such as F form polar bonds with the bonding pair further from the central atom; these bonding pairs are thus less repulsive than bonding pairs associated with less polar bonds. Thus in PF_2Cl_3, the F atoms will occupy axial positions.

Dipole Moments. An electric dipole is neutral overall, but has the positive and negative charges, $+q$ and $-q$, separated by distance r; the dipole aligns in an electric field. The dipole moment is defined by

$$\mu = |q| \, r \qquad (8\text{-}5)$$

Heteronuclear diatomic molecules like CO have dipole moments because of the difference in electronegativity of the C and O atoms. CO molecules tend to align in an electric field, and this response is experimentally measurable.

In general, the bonds between dissimilar atoms in polyatomic molecules are polar, so we can speak of a *bond dipole*. The dipole moment of the molecule as a whole is the vector sum of the individual bond dipoles. Thus we can compute the dipole moment of CF_3Cl, with approximate 109.5° bond angles, in terms of the CF and CCl bond dipoles,

$$\mu = \mu_{Cl} + 3\,\mu_{CF} \cos 109.5° = \mu_{Cl} + 3\,\mu_{CF}(-1/3) = \mu_{Cl} - \mu_{CF}$$

On the other hand, CF_4, with four polar CF bonds has no net dipole moment, since

$$\mu = \mu_{CF} + 3\,\mu_{CF} \cos 109.5° = \mu_{CF} + 3\,\mu_{CF}(-1/3) = 0$$

Molecules with unshared electron pairs on one side of the molecule, e.g., H_2O and NH_3, have larger dipole moments than would have been expected from bond polarity alone. The unshared electrons contribute significantly to the molecular dipole moment.

Isomerism

There are many examples of two or more distinctly different molecules which have the same molecular formula. Such molecules are called *isomers*. Three categories of isomerism are described below.

Structural Isomers. One kind of isomerism occurs when the atoms are connected in different ways. For example, three different structures can be drawn for the hydrocarbon C_5H_{12}, which differ in the carbon skeleton of the molecules, as shown in Figure 8-7. The first of these structural isomers, *pentane*, has 2 methyl groups (-CH_3) and 3 methylene groups (-CH_2-); the second, *2-methylbutane*, has 3 methyl groups, methylene, and a CH unit; and the third, *2,2-dimethyl-propane*, has 4 methyl groups and a single C atom to which these are bonded.

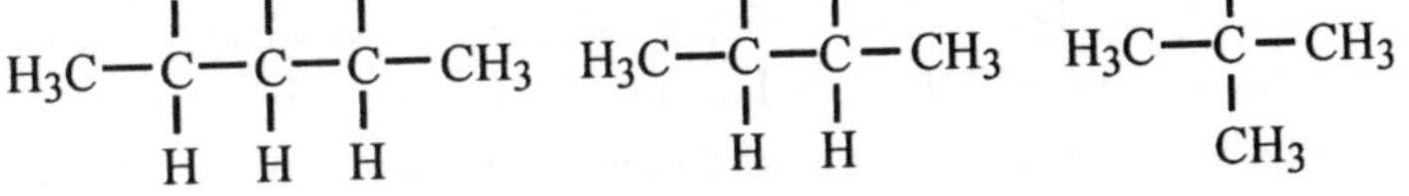

Figure 8-7. Structural isomers of C_5H_{12}.

Dichlorobenzene has three structural isomers, termed *ortho* (Cl atoms on adjacent C's), *meta* (Cl atoms on alternate C's) and *para* (Cl atoms on opposite C's). The *para* isomer is nonpolar and the *ortho* isomer has a large dipole moment; the *meta* isomer is intermediate in polarity.

Geometrical Isomers. In some isomers, the connections of the atoms is the same, but the isomers differ because at least two atoms, bonded to the same or adjacent atoms but not to each other, are at different distances from one another. Such isomers are termed *geometrical isomers*. Some examples are shown in Figure 8-8.

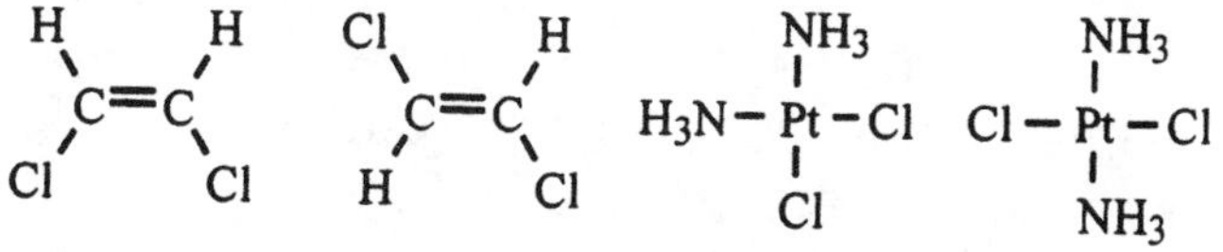

Figure 8-8. Examples of geometrical isomers.

ClHC=CHCl, *1,2-dichloroethylene*, has two geometrical isomers which we term *cis-* (Cl atoms on the same side) and *trans* (Cl atoms on opposite sides). Similarly, $Pt(NH_3)_2Cl_2$ has *cis* and *trans* isomers. The *cis* isomers have dipole moments (the polar C-Cl bonds have bond moments which add vectorially), but the *trans* isomers are nonpolar (the C-Cl bond moments cancel).

Optical Isomers. When a molecule can be assembled such that all the atom connections are the same, but with arrangements in space such that one isomer is the nonsuperimposable mirror image of the other, the isomers are called *optical isomers*. Most of the chemical and physical properties of optical isomers are identical, but the two isomers interact with polarized light differently, hence the name. Many molecules of biochemical relevance are optical isomers, with one isomer biologically active, the other inactive. The amino acid alanine (amino acids are the building blocks of proteins), shown in Figure 8-9, has two mirror image isomers.

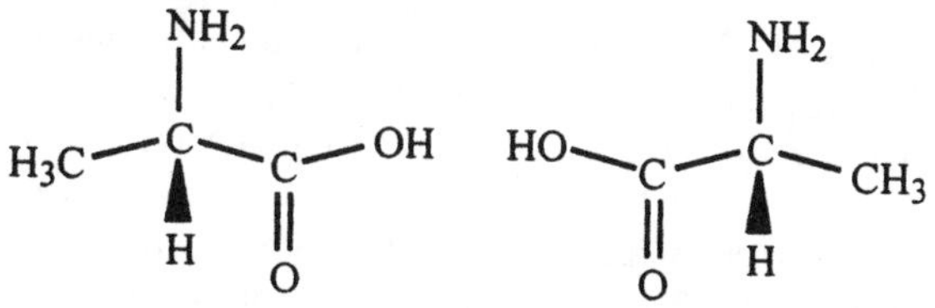

Figure 8-9. Optical isomers of the amino acid alanine.

A tetrahedral atom with four different groups bonded to it, as is the case with alanine, always results in a pair of optical isomers. Although there are other ways of arranging atoms as mirror images, the case of a tetrahedral C with four different groups is by far the most common.

Three Kinds of Isomerism:

- **Structural isomers differ in atom connectivity.**

- **Geometrical isomers have the same atom connectivity, but some atoms are arranged differently in space.**

- **Optical isomers are nonsuperimposable mirror images of one another.**

Problems

8.1 Draw Lewis structures of (a) CH_4O, (b) C_2H_3F, (c) N_3^-.

$$\text{(a) } H-\overset{\overset{\displaystyle H}{|}}{\underset{\underset{\displaystyle H}{|}}{C}}-\ddot{\underset{..}{O}}-H \qquad \text{(b) } \overset{H}{\underset{H}{>}}C=C\overset{H}{\underset{:\ddot{F}:}{<}}$$

Ans. $\text{(c) } \left[:\ddot{N}=N=\ddot{N}: \right]^- \longleftrightarrow \left[:\ddot{N}-N\equiv N: \right]^- \longleftrightarrow \left[:N\equiv N-\ddot{N}: \right]^-$

8.2 The dipole moment of LiH is 1.964×10^{-29} C m, and the LiH distance is 159.6 pm. What is the approximate percent ionic character in LiH? *Hint:* First calculate the dipole moment assuming 100% ionic character, with a charge at the center of each atom equal in magnitude to that of the electric charge, 1.602×10^{-19} C.
Ans. 76.8%

8.3 The dipole moments of SO_2 and CO_2 are 5.37×10^{-30} C•m and 0, respectively. What can be said of the shapes of the two molecules? *Ans.* CO_2 is linear, SO_2 bent.

8.4 The bond length in N_2^+ is 2 pm greater than in N_2 while the bond length in NO^+ is 9 pm less than in NO. Explain.

Ans. N_2 loses an electron from π_{2p}, NO loses an electron from π_{2p}^*

8.5 Given that ΔH_f° for H(g) is 218 kJ/mol, determine the H-H bond energy. *Ans.* 436 kJ/mol

8.6 Estimate ΔH for the reaction

$$C_2H_6(g) + Cl_2(g) \rightarrow C_2H_5Cl(g) + HCl(g)$$

given the average bond energies in kJ/mol, C-C (348), C-H (414), C-Cl (327), Cl-Cl (242), and H-Cl (431). ΔH is the sum of bond energies for bonds broken minus the sum of bond energies for bonds formed. *Ans.* −102 kJ/mol

8.7 Several resonance structures can be drawn for SO_4^{2-}: (i) 4 S-O single bonds (1 structure); (ii) 3 S-O bonds, 1 S=O (4 structures); (iii) 2 S-O bonds, 2 S=O bonds (6 structures); (iv) 1 S-O, 3 S=O (4 structures); and (v) 4 S=O (1 structure). (a) Determine the formal charge on S for each set of resonance structures. (b) Which set of resonance structures is likely to be most important?

Ans. (a) (i) +2, (ii) +1, (iii) 0, (iv) −1, (v) −2;
(b) set (iii) with 0 formal charge on S

8.8 Estimate the bond angles in (a) SCl_2, (b) NO_3^-, and (c) NO_2^-.
Ans. (a) < 109.5°, (b) 120°, (c) < 120°

8.9 Determine the steric number of the central atom and estimate (a) the Cl-P-Cl bond angle in $POCl_3$, (b) the F-I-F bond angles in IF_5, (c) the I-I-I bond angle in I_3^-.
Ans. (a) 4, <109.5°, (b) 6, <90°, (c) 5, 180°

8.10 Draw Lewis structures for all structural and geometrical isomers of C_4H_8.

Ans.

8.11 Draw Lewis structures for the structural isomers of C_4H_9Cl. Which of these is optically active (exists as a pair of optical isomers)? *Ans.* Isomer (b) is optically active

(a)

$$H-\overset{\overset{\displaystyle H}{|}}{\underset{\underset{\displaystyle H}{|}}{C}}-\overset{\overset{\displaystyle H}{|}}{\underset{\underset{\displaystyle H}{|}}{C}}-\overset{\overset{\displaystyle H}{|}}{\underset{\underset{\displaystyle H}{|}}{C}}-\overset{\overset{\displaystyle H}{|}}{\underset{\underset{\displaystyle H}{|}}{C}}-Cl$$

(c)

$$H-\overset{\overset{\displaystyle H}{|}}{\underset{\underset{\displaystyle H}{|}}{C}}-\overset{\overset{\displaystyle CH_3}{|}}{\underset{\underset{\displaystyle H}{|}}{C}}-\overset{\overset{\displaystyle H}{|}}{\underset{\underset{\displaystyle H}{|}}{C}}-Cl$$

(b)

$$H-\overset{\overset{\displaystyle H}{|}}{\underset{\underset{\displaystyle H}{|}}{C}}-\overset{\overset{\displaystyle H}{|}}{\underset{\underset{\displaystyle H}{|}}{C}}-\overset{\overset{\displaystyle H}{|}}{\underset{\underset{\displaystyle Cl}{|}}{C}}-\overset{\overset{\displaystyle H}{|}}{\underset{\underset{\displaystyle H}{|}}{C}}-H$$

(d)

$$H-\overset{\overset{\displaystyle H}{|}}{\underset{\underset{\displaystyle H}{|}}{C}}-\overset{\overset{\displaystyle CH_3}{|}}{\underset{\underset{\displaystyle Cl}{|}}{C}}-\overset{\overset{\displaystyle H}{|}}{\underset{\underset{\displaystyle H}{|}}{C}}-H$$

8.12 Draw the structures of the geometrical isomers of $Rh(NH_3)_3Cl_3$. *Ans.* Two isomers, one with each Cl *trans* to NH_3 (*facial* isomer), one with 1 Cl *trans* to NH_3 (*meridional* isomer)

8.13 Ethylene diamine, $H_2N-CH_2-CH_2-NH_2$ (en), is a *bidentate* ligand (two "teeth") which can bind to a metal with both N atoms. Draw structures of the geometrical isomers of $[Cr(en)_2Cl_2]^+$. Which of these is optically active? *Ans.* 2 isomers with Cl atoms *cis* and *trans*, *cis* isomer is optically active

8.14 The As-Cl bond distance in $AsCl_3$ is 217 pm. Estimate the single-bond covalent radius of As. *Ans.* 118 pm

8.15 Assuming C-C and C-Cl distances of 140 and 176 pm, what are the Cl-Cl distances in *ortho-*, *meta-*, and *para-*dichlorobenzene. Assume a perfect hexagon with C-Cl bonds lying on lines through the hexagon. *Ans.* 316 (*o*), 547 (*m*), 632 (*p*) pm

Chapter 9
SOLIDS AND LIQUIDS

IN THIS CHAPTER:

✔ *Interactions between Particles*
✔ *Crystals*
✔ *Liquids and Glasses*

Interactions between Particles

Since chemical species in condensed phases interact strongly, solids and liquids are more complicated than gases, where intermolecular forces are usually negligible. The interactions of atoms, molecules, and ions are *electrostatic* in origin, but there are several types of interaction with quite different energies:

Ion-ion interactions involve by far the largest energies. When like charges interact (a repulsive interaction), the energy is positive. When unlike charges interact (an attractive interaction), the energy is negative. These interactions are most important in ionic crystals.

Ion-dipole interactions are next in order of interaction energy. Such interactions are exemplified by the *solvation of ions* such as Na^+ and Cl^- by water. Water has a large dipole moment and H_2O molecules are strongly attracted to Na^+ with the negative end (O) of the water dipoles oriented toward the cation. Similarly Cl^- is solvated with the positive end of the water dipole (H) oriented toward the anion.

Dipole-dipole interactions are responsible for the cohesion of dipolar liquids. For example, methyl ether, CH_3OCH_3, with a dipole moment, boils at $-25°C$, but propane, $CH_3CH_2CH_3$, with about the same molar mass but negligible dipole moment, boils at $-45°C$.

Dipole–induced dipole interactions are also important. Nonpolar molecules tend to have their electron clouds attracted (or repelled) by a nearby dipolar molecule oriented with its positive (or negative) end toward the nonpolar species. This induced dipole interacts, on the average, with the dipolar molecule as if it were a permanent dipole. This effect is responsible for the solubility of nonpolar gases such as O_2, N_2, or CO_2 in water.

Induced dipole–induced dipole interactions, also called *London forces*, result when a nonpolar molecule undergoes a distortion, perhaps as a result of a collision, which results in a momentary separation of the centers of positive and negative charge. The resulting dipole induces a dipole in a neighboring molecule, resulting in an attractive interaction.

Both dipole–induced dipole and induced dipole–induced dipole interactions generally increase with number of electrons, particularly in atoms on the outer surface of the molecule. For example, the boiling points of the inert gases—He (4 K), Ne (27 K), Ar (88 K), Kr (120 K), and Xe (166 K)—increase with the number of polarizable electrons. UF_6 (bp $56°C$) is more volatile than $SbCl_5$ (bp $79°C$); uranium has more electrons than antimony, but the halogens are on the surface of the molecules, and there are more polarizable electrons in the five Cl atoms than in the six F atoms.

Dipole-dipole, dipole–induced dipole, and induced dipole–induced dipole interactions are often referred to collectively as *van der Waals interactions*.

Some dipolar molecules exhibit much greater intermolecular interactions than might have been expected from their dipole moments alone. This effect is illustrated by the data of Table 9-1.

Cmpd.	bp, K	Cmpd.	bp, K	Cmpd.	bp, K	Cmpd.	bp, K
CH_4	112	NH_3	240	H_2O	373	HF	293
SiH_4	161	PH_3	186	H_2S	212	HCl	188
GeH_4	185	AsH_3	218	H_2Se	231	HBr	206
SnH_4	221	SbH_3	256	H_2Te	271	HI	238

Table 9-1. Boiling Points of Some Simple Hydrides

The heavier hydrides behave as expected, i.e., an increase in boiling point with number of polarizable electrons. However, NH_3, H_2O, and HF have anomalously high boiling points. This effect is due to *hydrogen bonding*, the tendency of hydrogen atoms bound to electronegative atoms to interact with unshared electron pairs on adjacent molecules.

Hydrogen bonding is expected for hydrides with a strongly electronegative central atom—N, O, and F—with unshared pairs of electrons which can interact with the positive hydrogen of an adjacent molecule. Water is by far the best former of hydrogen bonds since it has two unshared pairs and two H's. NH_3 (one unshared pair and three H's) and HF (three unshared pairs and one H) have only half the potential hydrogen bonds of H_2O.

Interparticle interactions decrease in the order:
ion-ion > ion-dipole >

van der Waals interactions:
dipole-dipole > dipole–induced dipole >
induced dipole–induced dipole.

Hydrogen bonds are very strong intermolecular interactions for $-NH_2$, $-OH$, and
$-F$ groups.

Hydrogen bonds are not limited to NH_3, H_2O, and HF. Molecules containing $-NH_2$, $-OH$, or -HF groups are capable of hydrogen bonding. Hydrogen bonds are of great importance in many chemical and biochemical systems. The structure of ice depends on hydrogen bonds; the base pairing scheme of DNA vital to the genetic code relies on hydrogen bonds; the structures of proteins and many synthetic polymers are dictated by hydrogen bond formation.

Crystals

A piece of the crystal structure of NaCl, called the *unit cell*, is shown in Figure 9-1. The Cl⁻ ions are represented by shaded spheres, the Na⁺ ions by smaller white spheres. The unit cell is the smallest unit of the crystal which can be replicated to form the entire crystal. Thus if we duplicate the unit cell and superimpose the left-hand face of the duplicate on the right-hand face of the original, we have two unit cells of the crystal. If we do the same thing top to bottom, front to back, and continue many, many times, we will have the NaCl *lattice*.

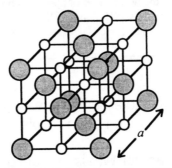

Figure 9-1. The Unit Cell of the Sodium Chloride Lattice

Notice that each Na^+ ion is surrounded by six Cl^- ions and each Cl^- ion is surrounded by six Na^+ ions. We say that the *coordination number* of Na^+ or Cl^- is 6, i.e., there are six nearest neighbor Cl^- or Na^+ ions around each Na^+ or Cl^- ion. There are 14 Cl^- ions, 8 at the corners and 6 centered on the faces; but only 13 Na^+ ions, 12 on the edges and 1 in the center of the unit cell. Ions on faces, edges, or corners are shared with the next cell. Ions on the corners are shared among 8 unit cells so that only 1/8 of each corner ion belongs to this unit cell. Similarly, ions centered on faces are shared by 2 cells so that 1/2 of each face ion belongs to this cell. Ions on edges are shared by 4 unit cells so that 1/4 of each edge ion belongs the this cell. An ion in the center belongs to this cell only. Revising the count, we have

$$\frac{8 \text{ corners}}{8} + \frac{6 \text{ faces}}{2} = \frac{4 \text{ Cl}^-}{\text{unit cell}} \qquad \frac{12 \text{ edges}}{4} + \frac{1 \text{ center}}{1} = \frac{4 \text{ Na}^+}{\text{unit cell}}$$

or four NaCl units per unit cell.

If we know the structure of a unit cell, we can use the molar mass and density to compute the dimensions of the unit cell. For example, NaCl (58.44 g/mol) has density 2.165 g/cm^3. The molar volume is:

$$\overline{V} = \frac{58.44 \text{ g/mol}}{2.165 \text{ g/cm}^3} = 26.99 \text{ cm}^3/\text{mol}$$

The volume of 4 NaCl units is the volume of one unit cell,

$$V_{cell} = \frac{4 \text{ NaCl}}{\text{cell}} \times \frac{26.99 \text{ cm}^3/\text{mol NaCl}}{6.022 \times 10^{23} \text{mol}^{-1}} = 1.793 \times 10^{-22} \text{cm}^3/\text{cell}$$

Taking the cube root, we have the unit cell dimension, $a = 5.639 \times 10^{-8}$ cm or 563.9 pm. The closest Na^+-Cl^- distance then is 281.9 pm. This distance can be regarded as the sum of the *ionic radii* of Na^+ and Cl^-. Using similar results from many other ionic crystals, the radii of many ions have been determined. A few of these are given in Table 9-2.

A unit cell is the smallest unit which can be replicated to form a crystal lattice.

Ion	r	Ion	r	Ion	r	Ion	r
Li^+	68	Be^{2+}	30	O^{2-}	145	F^-	133
Na^+	98	Mg^{2+}	65	S^{2-}	190	Cl^-	181
K^+	133	Ca^{2+}	94	Se^{2-}	202	Br^-	196
Rb^+	148	Sr^{2+}	110	Te^{2-}	222	I^-	219
Cs^+	167	Ba^{2+}	131				

Table 9-2. Some Ionic Radii in pm

Primitive Unit Cells. There are very many unit cell structures if we consider all the atoms or ions in the crystal. However, if we focus on just one atom or ion, we can reduce the number to just 14 *primitive cells*. Three of these, the *simple cubic, face-centered cubic (fcc)*, and *body-centered cubic (bcc)* unit cells, are shown in Figure 9-2. The lattice points, represented by small spheres in the drawings, correspond to the *centers* of the atoms, ions, or molecules occupying the lattice.

Following the procedure we used for NaCl, the number of atoms, ions, or molecules per unit cell is 1 for the simple cubic lattice, 4 for the fcc lattice, and 2 for the bcc lattice.

simple cubic   face-centered cubic   body-centered cubic

Figure 9-2. Three cubic unit cells.

Looking again at Figure 9-1, we see that the Cl⁻ ions form a fcc unit cell with the Na⁺ ions placed between each pair of Cl⁻ ions. Thus NaCl is a particular structure derived from the fcc primitive cell.

Cesium chloride crystallizes with a structure derived from the simple cubic primitive cell. Cl⁻ ions occupy the 8 corner sites with Cs⁺ in the center of the cell; note that this is <u>not</u> a body-centered cubic unit cell since the ion at the center is not the same as those at the corners. Thus there is one CsCl unit per unit cell and the coordination numbers of Cs⁺ and Cl⁻ are both 8. Crystals of CsBr and CsI adopt the CsCl structure, but all other alkali halides crystallize in the NaCl structure.

Closest packed structures. Consider an assembly of spherical atoms, placed in a layer with atoms touching as shown by the shaded circles in Figure 9-3 (layer A). A second layer of atoms can be laid down above the first layer as shown by the white circles (layer B). Placing the third and fourth layers over A and B gives the pattern ABABAB.... This arrangement is called *hexagonal closest packing* and the unit cell is shown in Figure 9-4.

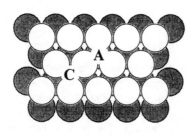   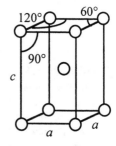

Figure 9-3.
Closest packing of spheres.

Figure 9-4.
Hexagonal unit cell.

The hexagonal unit cell is not cubic; the top and bottom are rhombuses and the vertical dimension is $c = \sqrt{8/3}\ a$. The top and bottom atoms are in layer A, the center atom in layer B. 1/6 of each atom at 120° corners is inside the unit cell, 1/12 of each atom at 60° corners is inside the unit cell; the atom in the center of course is entirely in the unit cell. Adding these up, we have 2 atoms/unit cell.

Returning to Figure 9-3, we could also place the third layer atoms over neither of the first two layers, so that one atom is a position C. More layers can be added, following the ABCABC . . . pattern. This arrangement, called *cubic closest packing*, has an fcc unit cell (the closest packed layers can be seen as planes of atoms perpendicular to the diagonal of the unit cell in Figure 9-2).

The fcc unit cell can be thought of as having holes in which other atoms or ions can be placed. For example, the Na^+ ions occupy *octahedral holes* in the fcc Cl^- lattice (connecting the six Cl^- ions surrounding a Na^+ by lines defines an octahedron). The fcc lattice also has *tetrahedral holes*; if we divide the unit cell into 8 smaller cubes, the centers of these little cubes are surrounded by 4 lattice points which define a tetrahedron. The diamond allotropic form of carbon has a fcc structure with C atoms in 4 of these tetrahedral sites; each C atom is surrounded by (covalently bound to) 4 other C's.

Liquids and Glasses

When a crystalline solid melts to a liquid, the regularity of the lattice is lost, but some local order may be retained. For example, in crystalline ice, each O atom is surrounded by four other O atoms linked by hydrogen bonds. In liquid water, the hydrogen bond network is partially retained, at least instantaneously, but long-range order is lost as the individual molecules are free to move about. Liquids with weaker intermolecular interactions are even more chaotic.

Don't Forget

Crystals are characterized by long-range order. Liquids and glasses are characterized by lack of long-range order. Most solids are polycrystals with frequent interruptions of order.

If we freeze a pure liquid very slowly, giving the atoms or molecules time to find their places in the lattice, a crystal grows. On the other hand, if we freeze the liquid quickly, the chaos of the liquid may be frozen in. The extreme case where there is no order at all is called a *glass*, often thought of as a *supercooled liquid*. Other solids may have regions of crystalline order, but lack long-range order.

Problems

9.1   Which liquid in the following pairs has the highest boiling point? Why?

(a) H_2O, H_2S; (b) $CH_3CH_2CH_2OH$, $HOCH_2CH_2OH$; (c) $CH_3CH_2CH_3$, CH_3CH_2F; (d) $CH_3CH_2CH_2CH_3$, CH_3CH_3

Ans. (a) H_2O, strong H-bonds,
(b) $HOCH_2CH_2OH$, twice as many H-bonds,
(c) CH_3CH_2F, dipole moment,
(d) $CH_3CH_2CH_2CH_3$, more polarizable electrons

9.2   Why does H_2O dissolve in acetone, CH_3COCH_3, but not in hexane, $CH_3CH_2CH_2CH_2CH_2CH_3$?

Ans. Acetone forms H bonds with water, hexane doesn't

9.3   Potassium crystallizes in a body-centered cubic lattice with $a = 520$ pm. (a) What is the distance between nearest neighbors? (b) How many nearest neighbors does each K atom have? (c) Compute the density of crystalline K.

Ans. (a) 450 pm, (c) 8, (c) 0.924 g/cm^3

9.4   KBr crystallizes with the NaCl structure. (a) Assuming additivity of ionic radii, what is the cell dimension a? (b) What is the smallest anion-anion distance?

Ans. (a) 658 pm, (b) 233 pm

9.5   The ZnS unit cell is a fcc lattice of S^{2-} ions with Zn^{2+} ions in alternating tetrahedral holes. (a) How many nearest neighbor S^{2-} ions does each Zn^{2+} have? (b) What angle is made by the lines connecting a Zn^{2+} with any two of its neighbors?

Ans. (a) 4, (b) 109.5°

9.6   Mg crystallizes in the hexagonal closest packed structure and has a density 1.74 g/cm^3. (a) What is the volume of the unit cell? (b) What is the distance between nearest neighbors? (c) How many nearest neighbors does each atom have?

Ans. (a) 4.64×10^{-23} cm^3, (b) 320 pm, (c) 12

Chapter 10
OXIDATION-REDUCTION

IN THIS CHAPTER:

- ✔ *Oxidation Numbers*
- ✔ *Nomenclature Based on Oxidation States*
- ✔ *Balancing Oxidation-Reduction Reactions*

Introduction

The term *oxidation* originally meant *reaction with oxygen* and *reduction* referred to the *production of a metal from an ore*. The terms have been modified and generalized over time so that chemists now think of these terms as follows:

Oxidation = electron loss

Reduction = electron gain

For example, $Fe \rightarrow Fe^{2+} + 2\ e^-$ represents the two-electron oxidation of iron and $Cl_2 + 2\ e^- \rightarrow 2\ Cl^-$ represents the two-electron reduction of Cl_2.

In both of these examples, the reactions are balanced not only in atoms but in charge where electrons, designated e⁻, are added to show that charge is conserved.

Oxidation Numbers

The degree of oxidation of an element is specified by the atom's oxidation number (ON), rules for which are as follows:

1. The oxidation number of a monatomic ion is the charge on the ion, e.g., for Fe^{2+}, ON(Fe) = +2, for Cl^-, ON(Cl) = –1. The alkali metals (Group IA) and alkaline earth metals (Group IIA) are always ionic in compounds like NaCl or $Mg(NO_3)_2$.
2. The ON of an uncombined element is 0, e.g., the ON is 0 for H in $H_2(g)$, S in $S_8(s)$.
3. The following conventions apply to covalently bound atoms: Except for the elements, (a) ON(F) = –1 (always); (b) ON(O) = –2 (except in peroxides like HOOH, where ON(O) = –1); (c) ON (H) = +1 (except in metal hydrides like NaH, where ON(H) = –1).
4. In molecules or ions containing two or more atoms, the sum of the ONs of all the atoms equals the charge on the species, e.g., H_2O: ON(O) + 2 ON(H) = –2 + 2(+1) = 0; to find ON(N) in NO_3^-: ON(N) + 3 ON(O) = –1, thus ON(N) = –1 –3(–2) = +5.

Example 1. What is the oxidation number of P in PO_4^{3-}?
In PO_4^{3-}, rule (4) gives
$$ON(P) + 4(-2) = -3 \qquad ON(P) = +5$$

Example 2. What is the oxidation number of Si in H_2SiO_3?
In H_2SiO_3, rule (4) gives:
$$2\ ON(H) + ON(Si) + 3\ ON(O) = 0$$
With rules (3b) and (3c), we have
$$2(+1) + ON(Si) + 3(-2) = 0 \qquad \therefore ON(Si) = +4$$
It is important to recognize that oxidation numbers are a bookkeeping device and should not be taken to indicate true charges or even formal charges. In H_2SiO_3—$SiO(OH)_2$—the Si-O and O-H bonds are covalent, i.e., electrons are shared between atoms; although we might expect the Si and H atoms to be somewhat positive and the O atoms somewhat negative, the charge separation is nowhere near as great as suggested by the ONs.

You Need to Know

Rules for assigning oxidation numbers (ONs):

- For monatomic ions, ON = charge
- Sum of ON's = 0 for molecules.
- Sum of ON's = net charge for ions.
- ON of an uncombined element = 0
- In combinations with other elements, ON(F) = –1 (always), ON(O) = –2 (usually)
- In combinations with other elements, ON(H) = +1 (usually).

Nomenclature Based on Oxidation States

Many metals exhibit two or more oxidation states. This is particularly true of the transition metals, where cations with ONs of +2 and +3 are common, but also of the heavier main-group metals such as thallium (ONs +1 and +3), and tin and lead (ONs of +2 and +4).

The modern system of nomenclature uses ONs directly in naming compounds. Thus in FeO and Fe_2O_3, the ONs of Fe are +2 and +3, respectively, and we name these compounds iron(II) oxide and iron(III) oxide. Similarly, phosphorus(III) cholride is PCl_3 and phosphorus(V) chloride is PCl_5.

The traditional nomenclature for salts of such metals is to use the suffix *-ic* for the higher ON and *-ous* for the lower, often using the Latin name for the element, e.g., ferrous (Fe^{2+}) and ferric (Fe^{3+}), stannous (Sn^{2+}) and stannic (Sn^{4+}), chromous (Cr^{2+}) and chromic (Cr^{3+}).

Monatomic and polyatomic anions containing a single element are named with the -ide suffix, regardless of the formal oxidation state, e.g., chloride (Cl^-), sulfide (S^{2-}), and triiodide (I_3^-).

Both metals and nonmetals form oxoanions with the central atom in a variety of oxidation states, e.g., NO_2^- and NO_3^-, MnO_4^{2-} and MnO_4^-. The traditional names reflect these differences by using the suffix -ate for the higher oxidation number and -ite for the lower. When more than two oxidation states are found, the highest uses the -ate suffix with the prefix per-, and the lowest uses the -ite suffix with the prefix hypo-. Some oxoanions with two central atoms linked by an oxygen use the di- prefix (indicating 2), others use the pyro- prefix, (indicating their origins as products obtained by heating—pyrolysis). Some of the more common polyatomic anions are listed in Table 10-1.

Table 10-1. Common Anions Exhibiting Variable ON's

Ion	Name	Ion	Name	Ion	Name
NO_2^-	nitrite	O^{2-}	oxide	ClO^-	hypochlorite
NO_3^-	nitrate	O_2^{2-}	peroxide	ClO_2^-	chlorite
PO_4^{3-}	phosphate	SO_3^{2-}	sulfite	ClO_3^-	chlorate
$P_2O_7^{4-}$	pyrophosphate	SO_4^{2-}	sulfate	ClO_4^-	perchlorate
VO_4^{3-}	vanadate	CrO_4^{2-}	chromate	MnO_4^{2-}	manganate
$V_2O_7^{4-}$	pyrovanadate	$Cr_2O_7^{2-}$	dichromate	MnO_4^-	permanganate

Balancing Oxidation-Reduction Reactions

There are two general approaches to balancing an oxidation-reduction reaction. Sometimes one is easier, sometimes the other, so it is best to master both. Both methods start with the same two steps:

1. Write a skeleton equation that includes major reactants and products. For aqueous solution reactions, $H_2O(l)$, $H^+(aq)$, $OH^-(aq)$, and spectator ions like $Na^+(aq)$ may be ignored at this stage.
2. Determine the oxidation numbers of all elements. Find out which element is oxidized and which is reduced. Determine the change in oxidation number.

At this point the two methods diverge.

Oxidation State Method:

3'. Electrons lost in the oxidation must be gained in the reduction. Thus adjust the stoichiometric coefficients to balance the changes in ONs.

4'. By inspection, supply the proper coefficients for the rest of the equation, adding $H_2O(l)$, $H^+(aq)$, or $OH^-(aq)$ as required.

Half-Reaction Method:

3". Write the oxidation and reduction half-reactions, adding electrons (e^-) on the right side of the oxidation half-reaction and on the left side of the reduction half-reaction to balance the changes in ON.

4". By inspection balance the half-reactions, adding $H_2O(l)$, $H^+(aq)$ or $OH^-(aq)$ as required. Adjust the coefficients in the two half-reactions so that the numbers of electrons are equal in each, and add the two half-reactions (the electrons cancel).

5". For either method, check the final equation to make sure that atoms *and* charge are balanced.

The rules by themselves are no doubt confusing. Let's see how they work with some examples.

Example 3. Balance the oxidation-reduction equation for the oxidation of $H_2S(aq)$ by $HNO_3(aq)$ to produce $NO(g)$ and $S(s)$ in aqueous acidic solution (thus H^+ and H_2O may be involved).

(1) $$NO_3^- + H_2S \rightarrow NO + S$$

(2) In NO_3^-, $ON(N) = +5$; in NO, $ON(N) = +2$, $\Delta ON = -3$. In H_2S, $ON(S) = -2$; in S, $ON(S) = 0$, $\Delta ON = +2$.

ON Method:

(3') Multiply the coefficients of N-containing species by 2 to get a 6-electron overall reduction; multiply the coefficients of S-containing species by 3 to get a 6-electron overall oxidation:

$$2 NO_3^- + 3 H_2S \rightarrow 2 NO + 3 S$$

(4') Balance O by adding 4 H_2O to the right; then balance H by adding 2 H^+ to the left:

$$2 H^+(aq) + 2 NO_3^-(aq) + 3 H_2S(aq) \rightarrow 2 NO(g) + 3 S(s) + 4 H_2O(l)$$

Half-Reaction Method:

(3") The oxidation and reduction skeletal half-reactions are:

$$H_2S \rightarrow S + 2 e^- \qquad NO_3^- + 3 e^- \rightarrow NO$$

(4") Balance half-reactions with H^+ and H_2O:

$$H_2S \rightarrow S + 2 e^- + 2 H^+ \qquad NO_3^- + 3 e^- + 4 H^+ \rightarrow NO + 2 H_2O$$

Multiply the coefficients of the first equation by 3 and the second by 2, and add, canceling the electrons:

$$3 \, H_2S \rightarrow 3 \, S + 6 \, e^- + 6 \, H^+$$
$$2 \, NO_3^- + 6 \, e^- + 8 \, H^+ \rightarrow 2 \, NO + 4 \, H_2O$$
$$3 \, H_2S + 2 \, NO_3^- + 8 \, H^+ \rightarrow 3 \, S + 6 \, H^+ + 2 \, NO + 4 \, H_2O$$

The H^+ also cancel in part, leaving

$$2 \, H^+(aq) + 2 \, NO_3^-(aq) + 3 \, H_2S(aq) \rightarrow 2 \, NO(g) + 3 \, S(s) + 4 \, H_2O(l)$$

(5) The two methods give the same result. Check that the atoms balance—2 N, 3 S, 6 O, and 8 H on each side—and that the charges balance—0 net charge on each side.

Essential Point

Balancing oxidation-reduction equations:

- Adjust coefficients so that ΔON (oxidation) + ΔON (reduction) = 0 or

- Adjust number of electrons in half-reactions so that electrons cancel when half-reactions add.

- Use H^+ & H_2O (acid solutions) or OH^- & H_2O (basic solutions) to balance H, O, and charge.

Example 4. Balance the oxidation-reduction equation for the oxidation of $FeCl_2$ by $Na_2Cr_2O_7$ to give $CrCl_3$ and $FeCl_3$ in aqueous acidic solution.

(1) $$Cr_2O_7^{2-} + Fe^{2+} \rightarrow Cr^{3+} + Fe^{3+}$$

(2) In $Cr_2O_7^{2-}$ and Cr^{3+}, $ON(Cr) = +6$ and $+3$, $\Delta ON = -3$; in Fe^{2+} and Fe^{3+}, $ON(Fe) = +2$ and $+3$, $\Delta ON = +1$.

ON Method:

(3') With two Cr atoms, total $\Delta ON(Cr) = -6$, $\Delta ON(Fe) = +1$. Multiply the coefficients of Fe species by 6.

(4') Balance O by adding 7 H_2O to the right; then balance H by adding 14 H^+ to the left:

$$Cr_2O_7{}^{2-}(aq) + 6\ Fe^{2+}(aq) + 14\ H^+(aq)$$
$$\rightarrow 2\ Cr^{3+}(aq) + 6\ Fe^{3+}(aq) + 7\ H_2O(l)$$

Half-Reaction Method:

(3") The skeletal oxidation and reduction half-reactions are:

$$Fe^{2+} \rightarrow Fe^{3+} + e^- \qquad\qquad Cr_2O_7^{2-} + 6\ e^- \rightarrow 2\ Cr^{3+}$$

(4") Balance the reduction half-reaction with H_2O and H^+,

$$Cr_2O_7^{2-} + 6\ e^- + 14\ H^+ \rightarrow 2\ Cr^{3+} + 7\ H_2O$$

Multiply the oxidation half-reaction coefficients by 6 and add,

$$Cr_2O_7^{2-}(aq) + 6\ Fe^{2+}(aq) + 14\ H^+(aq)$$
$$\rightarrow 2\ Cr^{3+}(aq) + 6\ Fe^{3+}(aq) + 7\ H_2O(l)$$

(5) The atoms are balanced—2 Cr, 6 Fe, 7 O, and 14 H on both sides—and so are the charges—24 positive charges on each side. If desired, the spectator ions can be reinserted:

$$Na_2Cr_2O_7(aq) + 6\ FeCl_2(aq) + 14\ HCl(aq)$$
$$\rightarrow 2\ CrCl_3(aq) + 6\ FeCl_3(aq) + 2\ NaCl(aq) + 7\ H_2O(l)$$

Balancing oxidation-reduction equations for reactions occurring in aqueous acidic solutions is usually fairly straightforward since we can use H_2O to balance O, and then H^+ to balance H. In basic solution, the "wild cards" are H_2O and OH^-. This complicates balancing since both species contain H and O. The best approach in this case is to balance the charge with OH^- and then balance O and H with H_2O.

Example 5. Balance the oxidation-reduction equation for the oxidation of Zn(s) by $NaNO_3(aq)$ to produce $Na_2Zn(OH)_4$ and $NH_3(aq)$ in basic aqueous solution.

(1) $\qquad\qquad Zn + NO_3^- \rightarrow Zn(OH)_4^{2-} + NH_3$

(2) In Zn and $Zn(OH)_4^{2-}$, $ON(Zn) = 0$ and $+2$, $\Delta ON = +2$; in NO_3^- and NH_3, $ON(N) = +5$ and -3, $\Delta ON = -8$.

ON Method:

(3') Multiply the coefficients of Zn species by 4:

$$4\ Zn + NO_3^- \rightarrow 4\ Zn(OH)_4^{2-} + NH_3$$

(4') Balance charge by adding 7 OH^- to the left,

$$4\ Zn + NO_3^- + 7\ OH^- \rightarrow 4\ Zn(OH)_4^{2-} + NH_3$$

Balance O (and H) by adding 6 H_2O to the left:

$$4\ Zn + NO_3^- + 7\ OH^- + 6\ H_2O \rightarrow 4\ Zn(OH)_4^{2-} + NH_3$$

Half-Reaction Method:

(3") Skeletal oxidation and reduction half-reactions:

$$Zn \rightarrow Zn(OH)_4^{2-} + 2\ e^- \qquad\qquad NO_3^- + 8\ e^- \rightarrow NH_3$$

(4") Add OH^- to balance charges:

$$Zn + 4\ OH^- \rightarrow Zn(OH)_4^{2-} + 2\ e^- \qquad NO_3^- + 8\ e^- \rightarrow NH_3 + 9\ OH^-$$

Add 6 H_2O on the left of reduction half-reaction to balance O and H:

$$NO_3^- + 8\ e^- + 6\ H_2O \rightarrow NH_3 + 9\ OH^-$$

Multiply the coefficients in the oxidation half-reaction by 4 and add the two half-reactions, canceling the electrons:

$$4\ Zn + 16\ OH^- \rightarrow 4\ Zn(OH)_4^{2-} + 8\ e^-$$
$$NO_3^- + 8\ e^- + 6\ H_2O \rightarrow NH_3 + 9\ OH^-$$
$$4\ Zn + 16\ OH^- + NO_3^- + 6\ H_2O \rightarrow 4\ Zn(OH)_4^{2-} + NH_3 + 9\ OH^-$$

Canceling 9 OH^-, we have

$$4\ Zn + NO_3^- + 7\ OH^- + 6\ H_2O \rightarrow 4\ Zn(OH)_4^{2-} + NH_3$$

(5) The atoms are balanced—4 Zn, 1 N, 16 O, and 19 H on each side—and so are the charges—8 negative charges on each side. Spectator ions may then be reinserted:

$$4\ Zn(s) + NaNO_3(aq) + 7\ NaOH(aq) + 6\ H_2O(l) \rightarrow$$
$$4\ Na_2Zn(OH)_4(aq) + NH_3(aq)$$

Problems

10.1 Determine the oxidation number of the italicized element in (a) $K_4P_2O_7$; (b) $NaAuCl_4$; (c) $Na_5HV_{10}O_{28}$; (d) ICl; (e) OF_2; (f) Ba_2XeO_6; (g) $Ca(ClO_2)_2$. *Ans.* (a) +5, (b) +3, (c) +5. (d) +1, (e) +2, (f) +8, (g) +3

10.2 Balance the following equations (acidic aqueous solutions):
(a) $Sn(s) + O_2(aq) + HCl(aq) \rightarrow SnCl_2(aq) + H_2O(l)$
(b) $CuS(s) + HNO_3(aq) \rightarrow Cu(NO_3)_2 + S(s) + NO(g) + H_2O(l)$
(c) $FeCl_2(aq) + H_2O_2(aq) + HCl(aq) \rightarrow FeCl_3(aq) + H_2O(l)$
(d) $As_2S_5(s) + HNO_3(aq) \rightarrow H_3AsO_4(aq) + H_2SO_4(aq) + NO_2(g)$
(e) $MnO(s) + PbO_2(s) \rightarrow MnO_4^-(aq) + Pb^{2+}(aq)$
(f) $C_2O_4^{2-}(aq) + MnO_4^-(aq) \rightarrow CO_2(g) + Mn^{2+}(aq)$
Ans. (a) 2 Sn + O_2, (b) 3 CuS + 2 NO_3^-, (c) 2 Fe^{2+} + H_2O_2,

(d) $As_2S_5 + 40 NO_3^-$, (e) $2 MnO + 5 PbO_2$,
(f) $5 C_2O_4^{2-} + 2 MnO_4^-$

10.3 Balance the following equations (basic aqueous solutions):
(a) $Bi_2O_3(s) + NaOH(aq) + NaOCl(aq) \rightarrow NaBiO_3 + NaCl(aq)$
(b) $Fe(CN)_6^{3-}(aq) + Cr_2O_3(s) \rightarrow Fe(CN)_6^{4-}(aq) + CrO_4^{2-}(aq)$
(c) $CrI_3(aq) + Cl_2(aq) \rightarrow CrO_4^{2-}(aq) + IO_4^-(aq) + Cl^-(aq)$
(d) $Ag(s) + CN^-(aq) + O_2(aq) \rightarrow Ag(CN)_2^- + OH^-(aq)$
(e) $Co^{2+}(aq) + Na_2O_2(aq) \rightarrow Co(OH)_3(s)$

Ans. (a) $Bi_2O_3 + 2 OCl^-$, (b) $6 Fe(CN)_6^{3-} + Cr_2O_3$,
(c) $2 CrI_3 + 27 Cl_2$, (d) $4 Ag + O_2$, (e) $2 Co^{2+} + O_2^{2-}$

10.4 Balance the following equations (no water involved):
(a) $NaN_3(s) \rightarrow Na_3N(s) + N_2(g)$
(b) $Ca_3(PO_4)_2(s) + SiO_2(s) + C(s) \rightarrow CaSiO_3(s) + P_4(s) + CO(g)$
(c) $P_2H_4(g) \rightarrow PH_3(g) + P_4H_2(g)$

Ans. (a) $3 NaN_3 \rightarrow Na_3N + 4 N_2$,
(b) $2 Ca_3(PO_4)_2 + 6 SiO_2 + 10 C \rightarrow 6 CaSiO_3 + P_4 + 10 CO$
(c) $5 P_2H_4 \rightarrow 6 PH_3 + P_4H_2$

10.5 What volume of 0.0500 M $KMnO_4$ is needed to oxidize 25 mL of 0.0800 M $Na_2C_2O_4$ in the reaction of problem 10.2(f)?

Ans. 16.0 mL

Chapter 11
PROPERTIES
OF SOLUTIONS

IN THIS CHAPTER:

✔ *Vapor Pressure Lowering*
✔ *Boiling Point Elevation*
✔ *Freezing Point Depression*
✔ *Osmotic Pressure*

Introduction

Dilute solutions have several properties, which are determined by the concentration, but not the identity, of the solute: so-called *colligative properties*. The Latin root is the same one from which *college* and *colleague* are derived, with an implication of working together to an end that transcends the individual.

Vapor Pressure Lowering

The vapor pressure of a solvent over a solution of nonvolatile solutes is always less than that of the pure solvent at the same temperature. This general result is stated by *Raoult's law*:

$$P_A = X_A P_A^{\bullet} \qquad (11\text{-}1)$$

vwhere P_A is the vapor pressure of A over a solution with solvent mole afraction X_A and $P_A^{\bullet}$ is the vapor pressure of pure A at the same temperature. Raoult's law is usually obeyed by the solvent in a dilute solution. We can understand Raoult's law as a consequence of solute molecules or ions diluting the solvent so that the rate of escape into the vapor phase is reduced by the fraction of solute molecules replacing solvent at the liquid-vapor interface, presumably the same fraction as in the bulk solution.

A gas is ideal if the intermolecular interactions are negligible. Most gases behave ideally at low pressures and at temperatures well above the boiling point of the liquid. Liquids have large intermolecular interactions, but we can define an *ideal solution* as one in which solute-solute, solvent-solute, and solvent-solvent interactions are very nearly identical. Such solutions are relatively rare; the only examples are mixtures of very similar molecules, e.g., methanol (CH_3OH) and ethanol (C_2H_5OH), or benzene (C_6H_6) and toluene ($C_6H_5CH_3$). Aqueous solutions are always far from ideal since water-water interactions are so different from the interactions of other molecules. In an *ideal solution*, Raoult's law is obeyed by a volatile solute as well as the solvent.

Although a volatile solute B generally does not obey Raoult's law, its concentration and partial pressures are nonetheless proportional,

$$C_B = K_h P_B \qquad (11\text{-}2)$$

Eq. (11-2) is known as *Henry's law*. K_h is a property of the solute and is called the Henry's law constant. Henry's law is really a special case of equilibrium which we will discuss in more detail in Chapter 12.

Raoult's law is directly responsible for two other properties of dilute solutions: the elevation of the boiling point and the depression of the freezing point.

Boiling Point Elevation

Since the vapor pressure of the solvent is lowered by the presence of solutes, the temperature at which the vapor pressure equals atmospheric pressure (where the solution boils) is higher than for the pure solvent, as shown in Figure 11-1. Detailed calculations show that the increase in boiling point for a dilute solution is proportional to the total molal concentration of solutes:

$$\Delta T_{bp} = T_{bp} \text{ (solution)} - T_{bp} \text{ (pure solvent)} = K_{bp} m_{solutes} \qquad (11\text{-}3)$$

K_{bp} is the *molal boiling-point constant*, a property of the solvent and independent of the nature of the solutes; $m_{solutes}$ refers to the total concentration of independent solute particles whether they are neutral molecules or ions. Thus a 0.01 molal NaCl solution has a total solute concentration (Na^+ and Cl^-) of 0.02 mol/kg. Eq (11-3) is accurate for dilute solutions: For non-ionic solutes, this generally means less than 0.1 mol/kg; for ionic solutes, less than 0.01 mol/kg. For more concentrated solutions, the boiling point is increased but not precisely in proportion to the solute molality.

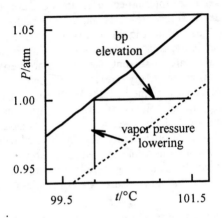

Figure 11-1. Liquid and vapor are at equilibrium along the vapor pressure curves shown for pure water (solid line) and an aqueous solution (dashed line). The vapor pressure is lower for the solution, in accord with Raoult's law, and thus the boiling point is increased (liquids boil at 1 atm)

A boiling point elevation measurement can be used to estimate the molar mass of a solute.

Example 1. 3.75 g of a nonvolatile solute was dissolved in 95 g of acetone. The boiling point was 56.50°C compared with 55.95°C for pure acetone. If K_{bp} = 1.71 K kg/mol for acetone, what is the approximate molar mass of the solute?

From Eq. (11-3), we have

$$m = \frac{\Delta T_{bp}}{K_b} = \frac{0.55 \text{ K}}{1.71 \text{ K kg/mol}} = 0.32 \text{ mol/kg}$$

The molar mass thus is

$$M = \frac{3.75 \text{ g}}{(0.32 \text{ mol/kg})(0.095 \text{ kg solvent})} = 1.23 \times 10^2 \text{ g/mol}$$

> ## Important to Know
> Boiling Point Elevation:
> $$\Delta T_{bp} = K_{bp} m_{solute}$$
> Freezing Point Depression:
> $$\Delta T_{fp} = K_{fp} m_{solute}$$
> K_{bp}, K_{fp} are constants, properties of the solvent.

Freezing Point Depression

When a solution freezes, the solid is usually pure solvent. Thus the solid-vapor equilibrium (sublimation) P-T curve is unaffected by the presence of solute. The intersection of this curve and the liquid-vapor curve is the *triple point* (nearly the same temperature as the freezing point, which is measured at atmospheric pressure). Since a solute lowers the solvent vapor pressure, the triple point is shifted to lower temperature, as shown in Figure 11-2. Detailed calculations show that the decrease in freezing point for a dilute solution is proportional to the total molal concentration of solutes

$$\Delta T_{fp} = T_{fp} \text{ (pure solvent)} - T_{fp} \text{ (solution)} = K_{fp} m_{solutes} \quad (11\text{-}4)$$

K_{fp} is the *molal freezing-point constant* of the solvent. Like K_{bp}, K_{fp} is a property of the solvent, independent of the nature of the solutes.

Example 2. The freezing point of pure camphor is 178.4°C and $K_{fp} = 40.0$ K kg/mol. Find the freezing point of a solution containing 1.50 g of a compound of molar mass 125 g/mol in 35.0 g of camphor.
The molality of the solution is

$$m = \frac{(1.50 \text{ g})/(125 \text{ g/mol})}{0.035 \text{ kg solvent}} = 0.343 \text{ mol/kg}$$

Thus
$$\Delta T_{fp} = (40.0 \text{ K kg/mol})(0.353 \text{ mol/kg}) = 13.7 \text{ K}$$
$$T_{fp} = 178.4 - 13.7 = 164.7°C$$

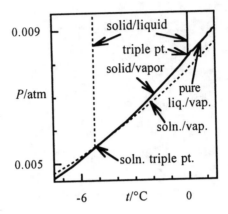

Figure 11-2. Solid-liquid, solid-vapor and liquid-vapor equilibrium curves for pure water (solid curves) and for a solution (dashed curves). The triple point (where solid, liquid, and vapor coexist and at nearly the same temperature as the freezing point) is shifted to lower temperature for the solution.

Osmotic Pressure

If a solution is separated from pure solvent by a *semipermeable membrane* that allows solvent, but not solute, molecules to pass through, solvent will move into the solution in an attempt to equalize the concentrations on the two sides of the membrane. This solvent transport process is called *osmotic flow*. If there is no resisting force, solvent will continue to flow into the solution until the solvent reservoir is exhausted. However, if the solutions are arranged as shown in Figure 11-3, the incoming solvent will force the solution up the extension tube. The weight of this solution in the tube exerts a downward pressure that tends to oppose the flow of solvent. Eventually this pressure will exactly balance the force of solvent flow and equilibrium is attained. This equilibrium pressure is called the *osmotic pressure*.

The osmotic pressure Π of a dilute solution of a nonelectrolyte is given by an equation formally equivalent to the ideal gas law:

$$\Pi = CRT \qquad (11\text{-}5)$$

If C is the molar concentration of solute, T in K and $R = 0.0821$ L•atm/mol•K, Π will have units of atm.

Osmotic pressure measurements are particularly convenient for determination of the molar mass of macromolecules such as proteins.

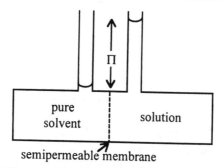

Figure 11-3. Osmotic Pressure Apparatus

When solvent can flow through a membrane impermeable to solute, the osmotic pressure is:

$$\Pi = CRT$$

Example 3. A solution was prepared by dissolving 0.750 g of crab hemocyanin in 125 mL of water. At 4°C, the osmotic pressure corresponded to a rise of 2.6 mm of the solution ($d = 1.00$ g/mL). Determine the molar mass of the protein.

We first convert the measured quantities to SI units and compute the osmotic pressure in pascals:

$$(2.6 \text{ mm})(10^{-3} \text{ m/mm}) = 2.6 \times 10^{-3} \text{ m}$$

$$(1.00 \text{ g/cm}^3)(10^{-3} \text{ kg/g})(100 \text{ cm/m})^3 = 1.00 \times 10^3 \text{ kg/m}^3$$

$$\Pi = (2.6 \times 10^{-3} \text{ m})(1.00 \times 10^3 \text{ kg/m}^3)(9.8 \text{ m/s}^2) = 25 \text{ Pa}$$

Then convert Π to atm and compute the concentration using eq (11-5):

$$\Pi = (25 \text{ Pa})/(101325 \text{ Pa/atm}) = 2.5 \times 10^{-4} \text{ atm}$$

$$C = \frac{\Pi}{RT} = \frac{2.5 \times 10^{-4 \text{ atm}}}{(0.0821 \text{ L•atm mol}^{-1}\text{K}^{-1})(277 \text{ K})} = 1.10 \times 10^{-5} \text{ mol/L}$$

Finally compute the molar mass:

$$M = \frac{m}{n} = \frac{m}{CV} \quad \frac{0.750 \text{ g}}{(1.10 \times 10^{-5}\text{mol/L})(0.125 \text{ L})} = 5.4 \times 10^{5} \text{ g/mol}$$

Problems

11.1 The vapor pressure of pure water at 28°C is 28.35 torr. Compute the vapor pressure of a solution containing 68 g of cane sugar, $C_{12}H_{22}O_{11}$, in 1 kg of water. *Ans.* 28.25 torr

11.2 At 30°C, pure benzene (C_6H_6) has a vapor pressure of 121.8 torr. Dissolving 15.0 g of a nonvolatile solute in 250 g of benzene produced a solution having a vapor pressure of 120.2 torr. What is the approximate molar mass of the solute?
Ans. 350 g/mol

11.3 Methanol (CH_3OH) and ethanol (C_2H_5OH) form a nearly ideal solution. At 20°C, the vapor pressure of methanol is 94 torr and that of ethanol is 44 torr. (a) Determine the partial pressure exerted by each component in a solution containing 20 g CH_3OH and 100 g C_2H_5OH. (b) What are the mole fractions in the vapor phase? *Ans.* (a) 21 and 34 torr, (b) 0.38 and 0.62

11.4 Compute the boiling point of a solution containing 24.0 g of a nonvolatile solute (molar mass = 58.0 g/mol) and 600 g of water when the barometric pressure is such that pure water boils at 99.725°C (K_{bp} = 0.513 K kg/mol for water). *Ans.* 100.079°C

11.5 A solution contained 10.6 g of a nonvolatile solute in 740 g of ether (K_{bp} = 2.11 K kg/mol) had a boiling point 0.284 K above that of pure ether. What is the approximate molar mass of the solute? *Ans.* 106 g/mol

11.6 A solution containing 4.50 g of a nonelectrolyte dissolved in 125 g of water freezes at –0.372°C (K_{fp} = 1.86 K kg/mol). What is the approximate molar mass of the solute?
Ans. 180 g/mol

11.7 Compute the approximate freezing point of a 0.015 molal solution of barium chloride, $BaCl_2$. *Ans.* –0.084°C

11.8 Compute the approximate freezing point of a 10% aqueous solution of methanol (CH_3OH). *Ans.* –6.5°C

Chapter 12
THERMODYNAMICS AND CHEMICAL EQUILIBRIUM

IN THIS CHAPTER:

✔ *Entropy and the Second Law of Thermodynamics*
✔ *Chemical Equilibrium*
✔ *Le Chatelier's Principle*
✔ *Equilibrium Calculations*

Introduction

We encountered a statement of the *first law of thermodynamics* in Chapter 6: The change in the internal energy of a system ΔE is equal to the sum of heat, q, absorbed by the system from the surroundings plus the work, w, done upon the system.

$$\Delta E = q + w \tag{12-1}$$

In this chapter, we are concerned with spontaneous processes and equilibrium. Spontaneous change for a mechanical system always involves a decrease in potential energy, $\Delta E < 0$, but this criterion does not hold for chemical systems.

Entropy and the Second Law of Thermodynamics

When NH_4Cl goes into solution, the NH_4^+ and Cl^- ions leave the highly ordered environment of the crystal to enter the chaotic world of a solution. This *increase in disorder* is the driving force for the endothermic dissolution of NH_4Cl.

The state function which measures disorder is the *entropy*, S, and the *second law of thermodynamics* may be stated as follows: The entropy of the universe or of an isolated system always increases when a spontaneous irreversible process occurs; entropy remains constant in a reversible process, i.e., a process which remains at equilibrium for every step along the way,

$$\Delta S_{universe} \geq 0 \tag{12-2}$$

The distinction between reversible and irreversible processes is illustrated by the following example.

Example 1. Consider a mixture of liquid and solid benzene at its normal freezing point, 5.45°C. If the temperature is raised by a tiny amount, say to 5.46°C, the solid portion will gradually melt; if the temperature were decreased to 5.44°C, the liquid would gradually crystallize. Freezing and melting are *reversible processes* at 5.45°C.

It is possible to cool liquid benzene to a temperature below the normal freezing point, say to 2°C, without crystallization. The liquid is then said to be *supercooled*. If a tiny crystal of solid benzene is added, the liquid will crystallize *spontaneously* and *irreversibly*. Raising the temperature to 2.01°C (or even to 3°C) will not stop the crystallization. One would have to raise the temperature to above 5.45°C to restore the liquid state. The crystallization of liquid benzene at 2.00°C is an example of an irreversible process.

For a *reversible* process, the change in a system's entropy is:

$$\Delta S = q_{rev}/T \tag{12-3}$$

Since entropy is a state function, we can use a reversible process with the same initial and final states to calculate the entropy change that occurs in an irreversible process.

Eq. (12-2) gives us a criterion for spontaneity, but it is restricted to systems that are not in thermal or mechanical contact with the surroundings. A more useful criterion is based on the *Gibbs free energy*, *G*, defined by

$$G = H - TS \qquad (12\text{-}4)$$

Equation (12-2) leads to the following criterion for spontaneity for a process occurring at *constant temperature and pressure*, but with the system in thermal and mechanical contact with the surroundings: The Gibbs free energy decreases for a spontaneous (irreversible) process and remains constant for an equilibrium (reversible) process.

$$\Delta G_{T,P} = \Delta H - T\,\Delta S \leq 0 \qquad (12\text{-}5)$$

G decreases for a spontaneous process, like the energy of a mechanical system. Since ΔG incorporates both driving forces for spontaneity—enthalpy (energy) decrease and entropy (disorder) increase—an endothermic process may be spontaneous if the increase in disorder is big enough to counteract the unfavorable enthalpy change, and a process that leads to increased order (negative ΔS) may be spontaneous if the process is sufficiently exothermic (negative ΔH).

The Second Law of Thermodynamics

A spontaneous process is predicted by:

- $\Delta S > 0$ for an isolated system,

- $\Delta G < 0$ for a system at constant *T* and *P*.

> ## Entropy change for a reversible process: $\Delta S = q_{rev}/T$

Example 2. Compute the entropy change when 1.00 g of ice is melted reversibly at 0°C, and when 1.00 g of liquid water is reversibly evaporated at 100°C.

Melting ice at 0°C ($\Delta H_{fus} = 334$ J/g):

$$\Delta S = \frac{q}{T} = \frac{(1 \text{ g})(334 \text{ J/g})}{273 \text{ K}} = 1.22 \text{ J/K}$$

Boiling water at 100°C ($\Delta H_{vap} = 2.26 \times 10^3$ J/g)

$$\Delta S = \frac{q}{T} = \frac{(1 \text{ g})(2.26 \times 10^3 \text{ J/g})}{373 \text{ K}} = 6.06 \text{ J/K}$$

Both processes lead to an increase in molecular disorder, and the entropy increases. When we freeze water or condense steam, the signs of q and ΔS are reversed, reflecting the increase in molecular order.

Example 3. Consider two 1-g pieces of iron ($C_p = 0.5$ J/g•K), one at 350 K, the other at 300 K. If the two pieces are put into thermal contact, heat will flow from the hot body to the cooler one. Calculate the total entropy change when the hotter body has been cooled to 349.9 K and the colder body has been warmed to 300.1 K.

Although the overall process is irreversible, as we shall see from the sign of ΔS, the change in entropy of each piece of iron is the same as if it had undergone the temperature change by reversible heat flow into or out of a heat reservoir, and eq (12-3) can be used for calculations.

If we cool the hot body reversibly from 350.0 to 349.9 K, the entropy change is

$$\Delta S = \frac{mC_p \, \Delta T}{T} = \frac{(1 \text{ g})(0.5 \text{ J/g K})(-0.1 \text{ K})}{350 \text{ K}} = -1.4 \times 10^{-4} \text{ J/K}$$

(Since the temperature change is so small, we can use the initial temperature in the denominator without serious error.) If the colder piece warms reversibly from 300.0 to 300.1 K, the entropy change is

$$\Delta S = \frac{mC_p \, \Delta T}{T} = \frac{(1 \text{ g})(0.5 \text{ J/g K})(+0.1 \text{ K})}{300 \text{ K}} = +1.7 \times 10^{-4} \text{ J/K}$$

If the two pieces of iron are placed in thermal contact and 0.05 J of heat allowed to flow, the overall entropy change is

Common Examples of Entropy:

- For a substance at the same temperature,

  $S_{solid} < S_{liquid} < S_{gas}.$

- Entropy of a gas increases with decreasing P.

- Entropy increases with increasing T.

- Entropy nearly always increases when a solute dissolves in a solvent.

- Entropy increases for a chemical reaction accompanied by an increase in the number of gas molecules or *neutral* molecules in liquid solution.

- Entropy usually decreases when a reaction occurs that increases the number of ions (ions interact strongly with the solvent and tend to increase order).

$$\Delta S_{total} = 1.7 \times 10^{-4} - 1.4 \times 10^{-4} = 3 \times 10^{-5} \text{ J/K}$$

$\Delta S > 0$ as expected for this spontaneous process.

The *Third Law of Thermodynamics* postulates that the entropy of a perfect crystal is zero at 0 K. Given the heat capacity and the enthalpies of phase changes, Eq. (12-3) allows the calculation of the *standard absolute entropy* of a substance, $S° = \Delta S$ for the increase in temperature from 0 K to 298 K. Some absolute entropies for substances in thermodynamic standard states are listed in Table 12-1.

Given standard absolute entropies and standard enthalpies of formation, one can compute *standard Gibbs free energies of formation*, $\Delta G_f°$. Just as for standard enthalpies of formation, $\Delta G_f°$ for elements in their most stable forms are, by convention, set equal to zero. Values of $\Delta G_f°$ are also given in Table 12-1.

Although enthalpies of substances are relatively independent of pressure (for gases) or of concentration (for dissolved species), entropies, and thus free energies as well, depend strongly on these variables. It can be shown that when the pressure of n mol of an ideal gas is changed from P_1 to P_2, or the concentration of n mol of the solute in an ideal solution is changed from C_1 to C_2, the entropy change is

$$\Delta S = nR \ln \frac{P_2}{P_1} \qquad \text{or} \qquad \Delta S = -nR \ln \frac{C_2}{C_1} \tag{12-6}$$

From these results, it is easy to show that, for a reaction

$$a\,A + b\,B \rightarrow c\,C + d\,D \tag{12-7}$$

the free energy change at any set of conditions, ΔG, is related to the standard state value, ΔG°, by:

for a gas-phase reaction: $\qquad \Delta G = \Delta G^\circ + RT \ln \dfrac{P_C^c\, P_D^d}{P_A^a\, P_B^b} \tag{12-8}$

$$\Delta G = \Delta G^\circ + RT \ln \frac{[C]^c[D]^d}{[A]^a[B]^b} \tag{12-9}$$
for a liquid-phase reaction:

Note that if the gases have partial pressures of 1 atm or the solution species have concentrations of 1 M, $\Delta G = \Delta G^\circ$. If ΔG is in joules, the gas constant R must be in J/mol•K.

Table 12-1. Standard Entropies (J/mol K)
and Free Energies of Formation (kJ/mol) at 298 K and 1 atm.

Substance	S°	ΔG_f°	Substance	S°	ΔG_f°
$Ag_2O(s)$	121.3	−11.21	$H_2(g)$	130.57	0
$Br_2(l)$	152.23	0	$H_2O(l)$	69.91	−237.18
$Br_2(g)$	245.35	3.14	$H_2O(g)$	188.72	−228.59
$C(s)$	5.74	0	$N_2(g)$	191.50	0
$CH_3OH)l)$	126.8	−166.35	$NO_2(g)$	239.95	51.29
$CH_3OH(g)$	239.7	−162.07	$N_2O_4(g)$	304.18	97.82
$C_2H_5OH(g)$	282.6	−168.57	$O_2(g)$	205.03	0
$CO(g)$	197.56	−137.15	$PCl_3(g)$	311.7	−267.8
$CO_2(g)$	213.63	−394.36	$PCl_5(g)$	364.47	−305.0
$Cl_2(g)$	222.96	0	$SO_3(s)$	52.3	−369.0
$Cl_2O(g)$	266.10	97.9	$SO_3(l)$	95.6	−368.4

Equations (12-8) and (12-9) are special cases of the more general relation

$$\Delta G = \Delta G^\circ + RT \ln Q \qquad (12\text{-}10)$$

where Q is the *reaction quotient*, which includes partial pressures (for gases) and concentrations (for solutes in liquid solutions) raised to a power equal to the stoichiometric coefficients for products (in the numerator) and reactants (in the denominator).

Example 4. Consider the synthesis of ammonia,

$$N_2(g) + 3\,H_2(g) \rightarrow 2\,NH_3(g)$$

$$\Delta G = \Delta G^\circ + RT \ln \frac{P_{NH_3}^2}{P_{N_2} P_{H_2}^3}$$

$\Delta G^\circ = -8.14$ kJ at 425 K. Suppose that we mix N_2 and H_2 at 425 K with initial partial pressures of 1.00 and 3.00 atm, respectively. Since there is no NH_3 initially, $\Delta G = -\infty$. As soon as some NH_3 is formed, the logarithm term becomes finite but still large and negative. For example, when the N_2 pressure has decreased to 0.90 atm, we have

$$\Delta G = -8.14 \text{ kJ} = (8.314 \times 10^{-3} \text{ kJ/mol K})(425 \text{ K}) \ln \frac{(0.20)^2}{(0.90)(2.70)^3}$$

$$= -29.67 \text{ kJ}$$

As the reaction proceeds, the NH_3 pressure increases as the partial pressures of N_2 and H_2 decrease. ΔG becomes less negative, eventually passing through zero to positive values as shown by Figure 12-1. Of course, when $\Delta G > 0$, the reaction is no longer spontaneous; indeed, NH_3 would dissociate to N_2 and H_2. When $\Delta G = 0$, there is no driving force in either direction, and the process has come to equilibrium, in this example when the partial pressures of N_2, H_2, and NH_3 are 0.29, 0.88, and 1.41 atm, respectively.

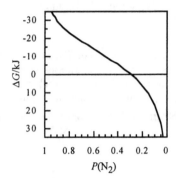

Figure 12-1. ΔG for the NH_3 synthesis reaction at 425 K starting with 1 atm N_2 and 3 atm H_2.

Chemical Equilibrium

As seen in Example 4, equilibrium is attained when $\Delta G = 0$. Thus Eq. (12-10) becomes

$$0 = \Delta G^\circ + RT \ln Q_{eq}$$

or
$$\Delta G^\circ = -RT \ln Q_{eq} \qquad (12\text{-}11)$$

Equation (12-11) is a remarkable statement. It implies that Q_{eq}, the value of the reaction quotient under equilibrium conditions, depends only on thermodynamics quantities that are constant in the reaction—the temperature and the standard free energy change for the reaction at that temperature—and is independent of the actual starting concentrations of reactants or products. For this reason Q_{eq} is called the *equilibrium constant, K*, and Eq. (12-11) is rewritten as

$$\Delta G^\circ = -RT \ln K \qquad (12\text{-}12)$$

For a process under standard state conditions ($T = 298$ K, $P = 1$ atm), eq (12-3) leads to

$$\Delta G^\circ = \Delta H^\circ - T\,\Delta S^\circ \qquad (12\text{-}13)$$

Combining Eqs. (12-12) and (12-13), we have

$$\ln K = -\frac{\Delta H^\circ}{RT} + \frac{\Delta S^\circ}{R} \qquad (12\text{-}14)$$

ΔH° and ΔS° are temperature-dependent, but not strongly so. Thus if we plot $\ln K$ vs. $1/T$, we should get a straight line with slope $-\Delta H^\circ/R$. On the other hand, if we have measured an equilibrium constant for a chemical reaction at two different temperatures, eq (12-14) gives

At T_1:
$$\ln K_1 = -\frac{\Delta H^{\circ}}{RT_1} + \frac{\Delta S^{\circ}}{R}$$

and at T_2:
$$\ln K_2 = \frac{\Delta H^{\circ}}{RT_2} + \frac{\Delta S^{\circ}}{R}$$

Subtracting, we have a way of computing ΔH°:

$$\ln \frac{K_1}{K_2} = -\frac{\Delta H^{\circ}}{R}\left(\frac{1}{T_2} - \frac{1}{T_1}\right)$$

(12-15)

Example 5. Estimate the boiling point of PCl_3 at 1 atm.

The boiling point is the temperature at which $\Delta G = 0$ for the process, $PCl_3(l) \rightarrow PCl_3(g)$.

Since $\Delta G = \Delta H - T_{bp}\,\Delta S = 0$, $T_{bp} = \frac{\Delta H}{\Delta S}$

If we assume that ΔH and ΔS are both temperature independent, we can estimate T_{bp} by using ΔH° and ΔS°. From Tables 12-1 and 6-2,

$$\Delta S^{\circ} = S^{\circ}(PCl_3, g) - S^{\circ}(PCl_3, l) = 311.7 - 217.14 = 94.6 \text{ J/K}$$

$$\Delta H^{\circ} = \Delta H_f^{\circ}(PCl_3, g) - \Delta H_f^{\circ}(PCl_3, l) = -287.0 - (-319.7) = 32.7 \text{ kJ}$$

$$T_{bp} \cong \frac{\Delta H^{\circ}}{\Delta S^{\circ}} = \frac{32.7 \times 10^3 \text{ J}}{94.6 \text{ J/K}} = 346 \text{ K}$$

Example 6. When $O_2(g)$ at 1.00 atm pressure is equilibrated with pure water, some O_2 dissolves: $[O_2] = 0.0017$ M at 10°C and 0.0010 M at 40°C. What are ΔH° and ΔS° for the process, $O_2(g) \rightarrow O_2(aq)$?

The equilibrium constant expression for this process is

$$K = \frac{[O_2]}{P_O}$$

with $K = 0.0017$ at 283 K, 0.0010 at 313 K (the standard states for $O_2(aq)$ and $O_2(g)$ are 1 M and 1 atm, respectively). Note that this equilibrium constant expression is Henry's law (see Chapter 11). Substitution into eq (12-16) gives

$$\ln\frac{0.0017}{0.0010} = \frac{\Delta H^{\circ}}{8.314 \text{ J/mol K}}\left(\frac{1}{313 \text{ K}} - \frac{1}{283 \text{ K}}\right)$$

$$0.53 = (-4.07 \times 10^{-5} \text{ mol/J}) \, \Delta H°$$

and $\Delta H° = -13 \times 10^3$ J/mol. We now compute $\Delta G°$ at 283 K,

$$\Delta G° = -RT \ln K$$

$$\Delta G° = -(8.314 \text{ J/mol K})(283 \text{ K}) \ln(0.0017) = +15 \times 10^3 \text{ J/mol}$$

Then use Eq. (12-13) to compute $\Delta S°$:

$$\Delta G° = \Delta H° - T \, \Delta S°$$

$$15 \times 10^3 \text{ J/mol} = -13 \times 10^3 \text{ J/mol} - (283 \text{ K}) \, \Delta S°$$

$$\Delta S° = -99 \text{ J/mol·K}$$

The solution of O_2 in water is energetically favorable ($\Delta H° < 0$), but the highly unfavorable entropy leads to positive $\Delta G°$ and a small equilibrium constant.

Le Chatelier's Principle:

If a stress is brought to bear on a system in equilibrium, a reaction will occur in the direction which tends to relieve the stress.

Le Chatelier's Principle

Henri Le Chatelier was responsible for a general principle which is very useful in predicting the qualitative effect of changes in temperature, pressure, or concentration upon a system at equilibrium:

Change in Partial Pressure or Concentration. Consider the gas-phase equilibrium,

$$CO(g) + 2 H_2(g) \rightleftarrows CH_3OH(g)$$

If we add more CO and so increase P_{CO}, Le Chatelier's principle states that the system will respond in such a way as to decrease P_{CO}. It does this by reacting to consume CO, producing more CH_3OH (and incidentally consuming H_2). A similar argument applies to solution-phase equilibrium: increasing the concentration of one species will shift the equilibrium to consume that species.

Effect of Dilution or Volume Change. Suppose we increase the volume of the above gas-phase equilibrium. The total pressure will decrease, and, according to Le Chatelier's principle, the system will

Predictions Based on Le Chatelier's Principle:

- Increasing the concentration or pressure of one component of an equilibrium leads to a reaction that consumes that component.

- Increasing the volume of a gas equilibrium or adding solvent to a solution equilibrium leads to a reaction that produces more molecules.

- Increasing the temperature of an equilibrium system causes a reaction that absorbs heat.

respond to increase the total pressure. Since 3 mol of reactants is converted to 1 mol of products, a forward reaction decreases the total pressure, a reverse reaction increases the total pressure. Thus the equilibrium will shift to the left. Similarly a decrease in volume would lead to a shift to the right, forming more CH_3OH. A similar argument applies to the dilution of a solution-phase equilibrium.

Effect of Changes in Temperature. When the temperature of a system at equilibrium is increased, a reaction occurs in the direction that absorbs heat. The above equilibrium is exothermic when the reaction proceeds to the right, $\Delta H° = -90$ kJ. Thus if the temperature is increased, we expect the equilibrium to shift such as to absorb heat. Shifting to the right would liberate more heat, thus we expect a shift toward CO and H_2. This conclusion can also be based on Eq. (12-14). Since $\Delta H°$ is negative, an increase in temperature will decrease K, i.e., shift the equilibrium to the left

Effect of Catalysts. A catalyst is a substance which increases the rate of a reaction. When a reaction is reversible, a catalyst increases both the forward and reverse reaction, leaving the equilibrium constant unaffected. Thus addition of a catalyst will cause a reaction to reach equilibrium faster, but it will not affect the position of equilibrium.

Equilibrium Calculations

With an equilibrium constant expression and a numerical value for K, we can compute the composition of an equilibrium mixture. Problems are often stated in terms of initial amounts of products and/or reactants. It is usually convenient to set up a table with a column for each reactant and product species, entering (i) the initial concentrations or partial pressures; (ii) the change in each concentration or pressure in terms of an unknown x; and (iii) the equilibrium concentrations or partial pressures in terms of x. Substitution of the expressions in row (iii) into the equilibrium constant expression leads to an equation in x, the root of which allows calculations of the equilibrium concentrations or partial pressures. The procedure is best illustrated by examples.

Example 7. When 1.0 mol of PCl_5 is heated in a 10-L vessel to 250°C, it dissociates according to

$$PCl_5(g) \rightleftarrows PCl_3(g) + Cl_2(g)$$

Calculate the partial pressures of PCl_5, PCl_3, and Cl_2 at equilibrium given that $K = 1.8$ at 250°C.

Calculate the initial partial pressure of PCl_5 and set up a table:

Initially,
$$P(PCl_5) = \frac{nRT}{V} = \frac{1.0 \text{ mol}}{10 \text{ L}} \times 0.082 \text{ L atm mol}^{-1}\text{K}^{-1} \times 523 \text{ K} = 4.3 \text{ atm}$$

	$P(PCl_5)$	$P(PCl_3)$	$P(Cl_2)$
initial	4.3 atm	0.0 atm	0.0 atm
change	$-x$	$+x$	$+x$
equilibrium	$4.3 - x$	x	x

Substituting into the equilibrium constant expression,

$$K = \frac{P_{PCl_3} P_{Cl_2}}{P_{PCl_5}} \qquad 1.8 = \frac{x^2}{4.3 - x} \qquad x^2 + 1.8x - 7.74 = 0$$

Solving the quadratic equation:

$$x = -\frac{1.8}{2} \pm \frac{1}{2}\sqrt{1.8^2 + 4 \times 7.74} = -0.9 \pm 2.9$$

The negative root makes no sense in this context, so we choose $x = 2.0$ so that $P(PCl_3) = P(Cl_2) = 2.0$ atm, $P(PCl_5) = 2.3$ atm.

Example 8. H_3P-BCl_3 dissociates to give PH_3 and BCl_3:

$$H_3P-BCl_3(s) \rightleftarrows PH_3(g) + BCl_3(g)$$

$$K = P_{PH3}\, P_{BCl3} = 0.052 \text{ at } 60°C$$

Since H_3P-BCl_3 is a solid, it remains in its standard state as long as there is any solid present and thus does not appear in the equilibrium constant expression. 500 mL of a gas mixture was prepared with 1.00 atm of PH_3 and 0.100 atm of BCl_3. Compute the equilibrium partial pressures at 60°C. What mass of H_3P-BCl_3 was formed?

	P_{PH3}, atm	P_{BCl3}, atm
initial	1.00	0.100
change	$-x$	$-x$
equilibrium	$1.00 - x$	$0.100 - x$

Substituting into the equilibrium constant expression, we have

$$0.052 = (1.00 - x)(0.100 - x)$$
$$x^2 - 1.100\, x + 0.0480 = 0$$

The quadratic equation has roots: $x = 1.054$ and 0.0455. Since neither pressure can be negative, we choose the latter root and have $P_{PH3} = 0.954$ atm, $P_{BCl3} = 0.054$ atm. The decrease in the partial pressures of PH_3 and BCl_3 corresponds to moles of H_3P-BCl_3 formed. Thus

$$n = -\frac{\Delta PV}{RT} = -\frac{(-0.0455 \text{ atm})(0.500 \text{ L})}{(0.0821 \text{ L atm/mol K})(333 \text{ K})} = 8.23 \times 10^{-4} \text{ mol}$$

$$m = (8.32 \times 10^{-4} \text{ mol})(151.2 \text{ g/mol}) = 0.126 \text{ g } H_3P-BCl_3$$

Problems

12.1 Without consulting entropy tables, predict the sign of ΔS for each of the following processes:

(a) $O_2(g) \rightarrow 2\, O(g)$ *Ans.* +
(b) $N_2(g) + 3\, H_2(g) \rightarrow 2\, NH_3(g)$ *Ans.* −
(c) $C(s) + H_2O(g) \rightarrow CO(g) + H_2(g)$ *Ans.* +
(d) $Br_2(l) \rightarrow Br_2(g)$ *Ans.* +
(e) $N_2(g, 10 \text{ atm}) \rightarrow N_2(g, 1 \text{ atm})$ *Ans.* +
(f) $NH_3(aq) + H_2O(l) \rightarrow NH_4^+(aq) + OH^-(aq)$ *Ans.* −
(g) $C_6H_{12}O_6(s) \rightarrow C_6H_{12}O_6(aq)$ *Ans.* +

12.2 Using the data of Table 12-1, compute (a) ΔS°, (b) ΔH° for the reaction, $2\,C(s) + 3\,H_2(g) + \frac{1}{2}\,O_2(g) \rightarrow C_2H_5OH(g)$, at 298 K.
Ans. (a) -223.1 J/K, (b) -235.08 kJ

12.3 (a) Compute ΔS° and ΔG° for the reaction at 298 K,
$$H_2(g) + CO_2(g) \rightarrow H_2O(g) + CO(g)$$
(b) Compute ΔG for the above reaction at 298 K when the partial pressures of H_2, CO_2, H_2O, and CO are 10, 20, 0.02, and 0.01 atm, respectively.
(c) Compute the equilibrium constant K for the above reaction at 298 K. *Ans.* (a) 42.08 J/K, 28.62 kJ, (b) -5.61 kJ, (c) 9.62×10^{-6}

12.4 SO_3 decomposes on heating: $2\,SO_3(g) \rightleftarrows 2\,SO_2(g) + O_2(g)$. A sample of pure SO_3 was heated to a high temperature T. At equilibrium, the mole ratio of SO_2 to SO_3 was 0.152 and the total pressure was 2.73 atm. (a) What is K? (b) If an amount of SO_3 equal to that present at equilibrium is added and the system allowed to come to equilibrium, what are the partial pressures of SO_3, SO_2, and O_2?
Ans. (a) 0.00390, (b) 4.26, 0.521, 0.261 atm

12.5 Calculate ΔH_f° for Cl_2O at 25°C. *Ans.* 80.2 kJ/mol

12.6 Under what conditions could the decomposition of Ag_2O into $Ag(s)$ and $O_2(g)$ proceed spontaneously at 25°C?
Ans. when the partial pressure of O_2 is less than 0.090 atm

12.7 Predict the effect upon the following reaction equilibria of (a) increased temperature (see Table 6-2), (b) increased pressure.

$CO(g) + H_2O(g) \rightleftarrows CO_2(g) + H_2(g)$ *Ans.* (a) R, (b) neither

$2\,SO_2(g) + O_2(g) \rightleftarrows 2\,SO_3(g)$ *Ans.* (a) R, (b) F

$N_2O_4(g) \rightleftarrows 2\,NO_2(g)$ *Ans.* (a) F, (b) R

$CaCO_3(s) \rightleftarrows CaO(s) + CO_2(g)$ *Ans.* (a) F, (b) R

$2\,O_3(g) \rightleftarrows 3\,O_2(g)$ *Ans.* (a) R, (b) R

$C(s,\ diamond) \rightleftarrows C(s,\ graphite)$ *Ans.* (a) R, (b) R
densities in g/cm³: 3.5 (diamond) and 2.3 (graphite)
(F = favors forward reaction, R = favors reverse reaction)

Chapter 13
ACIDS
AND BASES

IN THIS CHAPTER:

✔ *Definitions of Acids and Bases*
✔ *Ionization of Water and the pH Scale*
✔ *Strengths of Acids and Bases*
✔ *Acid-Base Equilibrium*

Definitions of Acids and Bases

Arrhenius definitions. In the 1880s, Svante Arrhenius defined acids and bases as substances that ionize in solution to produce H^+ and OH^- ions, respectively. We still often think of acids and bases in these terms, but the definitions can be misleading. For example, an aqueous solution of ammonia, NH_3, contains ammonium and hydroxide ions, NH_4^+ and OH^-; the Arrhenius definition suggests that these came from the ionization of NH_4OH, but there is no such compound.

Brönsted-Lowry definitions. The difficulty of fitting NH_3 into a general scheme of acids and bases was solved in 1923 by Johannes Brönsted and Thomas Lowry, who defined an acid as a proton donor and

113

a base as a proton acceptor. Thus NH_3 acts as a base and accepts a proton (H^+) from H_2O, and H_2O acts as an acid in donating a proton to NH_3.

$$NH_3(aq) + H_2O(l) \rightleftarrows NH_4^+(aq) + OH^-(aq) \qquad (13\text{-}1)$$

The reverse reaction is also an acid-base reaction: NH_4^+ acts as an acid in donating a proton to the base, OH^-. In the Brönsted-Lowry scheme, every acid has a conjugate base and every base has a conjugate acid. Thus NH_4^+ is the acid conjugate to the base NH_3, and OH^- is the base conjugate to the acid H_2O. Similarly, acetic acid, CH_3COOH, donates its acidic proton to H_2O to produce the conjugate base, acetate ion, $CH_3CO_2^-$:

$$CH_3COOH(aq) + H_2O(l) \rightleftarrows CH_3CO_2^-(aq) + H_3O^+(aq) \qquad (13\text{-}2)$$

Notice that water can act both as an acid, with conjugate base OH^-, and as a base, with conjugate acid H_3O^+.

Brönsted-Lowry Definitions of Acids and Bases:

- Acid = proton donor, base = proton acceptor.

- In the equilibrium, HA + B $\rightleftarrows$ A$^-$ + HB$^+$, HA/A$^-$, HB$^+$/B are conjugate acid-base pairs.

- Water can act either as an acid or as a base, producing OH$^-$ or H$_3$O$^+$.

Lewis definitions. General definitions of acids and bases were given by G. N. Lewis as an extension of the concept of the electron-pair covalent bond: an acid is an electron-pair acceptor, a base an electron-pair donor. All Lewis bases are Brönsted bases—an unshared electron pair is required to accept a proton. H^+ is an acid in the Lewis sense since it can accept an electron pair from a base such as NH_3, but H_2O and NH_4^+ are not Lewis acids. Metal ions act as Lewis acids when they accept an electron pair from Lewis bases such as NH_3 to form complex ions (Chapter 14). Other electron-deficient molecules such as BF_3 act as Lewis acids and form covalent bonds with bases like NH_3:

$$NH_3(g) + BF_3(g) \rightleftarrows H_3N\text{-}BF_3(s)$$

For most aqueous acid-base chemistry, the Lewis definitions are too general and lack the symmetry of the acid–conjugate base relationship. We will mostly use the Brönsted-Lowry definitions.

Lewis Definitions of Acids and Bases:

- A base is an electron pair donor,

- An acid is an electron pair acceptor.

Ionization of Water and the pH Scale

Every aqueous solution contains hydronium (H_3O^+) and hydroxide (OH^-) ions as a result of the water auto-ionization process,

$$2\ H_2O(l) \rightleftarrows H_3O^+(aq) + OH^-(aq) \quad K_w = [H_3O^+][OH^-] \qquad (13\text{-}3)$$
$$K_{w,298} = 1.00 \times 10^{-14}$$

$[H_2O]$ does not appear in the equilibrium constant expression since, in dilute solutions, H_2O is very close to the standard state condition of pure liquid. In pure water at 25°C, $[H_3O^+] = [OH^-] = K_w^{1/2} = 1.00 \times 10^{-7}$ M. Because the water ionization is endothermic, K_w increases with increasing T.

In 0.10 M HCl solution, HCl is completely ionized,

$$HCl(aq) + H_2O(aq) \rightarrow H_3O^+(aq) + Cl^-(aq)$$

and $[H_3O^+] = 0.10$ M, $[OH^-] = 1.0 \times 10^{-13}$ M. Similarly 0.10 M NaOH is completely ionized,

$$NaOH(aq) \rightarrow Na^+(aq) + OH^-(aq)$$

and $[OH^-] = 0.10$ M, $[H_3O^+] = 1.0 \times 10^{-13}$ M. Because of the enormous range in the concentrations of H_3O^+ and OH^- ions, we usually use a logarithmic scale to express these concentrations:

$$pH = -\log_{10}[H_3O^+] \quad [H_3O^+] = 10^{-pH} \tag{13-4}$$

$$pOH = -\log_{10}[OH^-] \quad [OH^-] = 10^{-pOH} \tag{13-5}$$

Since the H_3O^+ and OH^- concentrations are related by Eq. (13-3),

$$pH + pOH = pK_w = -\log_{10}K_w \tag{13-6}$$

(In general, $pX = -\log_{10}[X]$.) Thus, for 0.10 M HCl, pH = 1.00, pOH = 13.00, and for 0.10 M NaOH, pH = 13.00, pOH = 1.00.

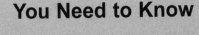

You Need to Know

Logarithmic scales used for concentrations and equilibrium constants:

- $pH = -\log_{10}[H_3O^+]$

- $pOH = -\log_{10}[OH^-]$

- $pK_w = -\log_{10}K_w$

- $pK_a = -\log_{10}K_a$

Water is not unique in undergoing auto-ionization. Several other solvents are capable of acting both as acids and bases, e.g., the following equilibrium occurs in liquid ammonia (bp $-33°C$):

$$2\ NH_3(l) \rightleftarrows NH_4^+(am) + NH_2^-(am)$$

Strengths of Acids and Bases

The equilibria of Eqs. (13-1) and (13-2) correspond to the equilibrium constant expressions:

$$K_b = \frac{[NH_4^+][OH^-]}{[NH_3]} \qquad (13\text{-}7)$$

$$K_a = \frac{[H_3O^+][CH_3CO_2^-]}{[CH_3COOH]} \qquad (13\text{-}8)$$

These expressions are often written in logarithmic form:

$$pOH = pK_b + \log_{10}\frac{[NH_4^+]}{[NH_3]} \qquad (13\text{-}9)$$

$$pH = pK_a + \log_{10}\frac{[CH_3CO_2^-]}{[CH_3COOH]} \qquad (13\text{-}10)$$

We can also think of NH_4^+ as an acid, so that in solutions of NH_4Cl, we have the equilibrium

$$NH_4^+(aq) + H_2O(l) \rightleftarrows H_3O^+(aq) + NH_3(aq)$$

$$K_a = \frac{[H_3O^+][NH_3]}{[NH_4^+]}$$

or
$$pH = pK_a + \log_{10}\frac{[NH_3]}{[NH_4^+]} \qquad (13\text{-}11)$$

Adding eqs (13-9) and (13-11), we have

$$pH + pOH = pK_a + pK_b = pK_w; \text{ and } K_b = K_w/K_a \qquad (13\text{-}12)$$

Equation (13-12) is a general result relating pK_a of an acid with pK_b of the conjugate base.

The value of K_a or K_b (pK_a or pK_b) determines the extent of ionization of an acid or base. We think of strong acids or bases as completely ionized (or nearly so). This generally implies K_a or K_b greater than 1 (negative pK_a or pK_b). The pK_a values for several acids are given in Table 13-1.

Many common acids are *oxoacids*, i.e., molecules with the central atom surrounded by =O (oxo) and -OH (hydroxo) groups. Perchloric ($HClO_4$), chloric ($HClO_3$), chlorous ($HClO_2$), and hypochlorous ($HClO$) acids can be written $ClO_3(OH)$, $ClO_2(OH)$, $ClO(OH)$, and $ClOH$, respectively, to emphasize the distinction between oxo and hydroxo oxygens. The acid strength increases with the number of oxo O's. The increased acidity results from the delocalization of negative charge in the anions as shown in Figure 13-1 for the Cl oxoanions. The average formal charge on oxygen is $-1/4$ in ClO_4^-, $-1/3$ in ClO_3^-, $-1/2$ in ClO_2^-, and -1 in ClO^-.

Table 13-1. pK_a's of Some Common Acids

Acid	pK_a	Acid	pK_a	Acid	pK_a
HF	3.45	HNO_3	−1.3	$HClO_4$	−7
HCl	−7	HNO_2	3.34	$HClO_3$	−3
HBr	−9	HCOOH	3.75	$HClO_2$	1.96
HI	−11	CH_3COOH	4.75	HClO	7.53
H_2SO_3	1.81	H_2CO_3	6.37	NH_4^+	9.25
	6.91		10.25	H_3PO_4	2.12
H_2SO_4	−2	$H_2C_2O_4$	1.23		7.21
	1.92		4.19		12.67

Figure 13-1. Resonance structures of the perchlorate, chlorate, chlorite, hypochlorite, formate, and nitrite ions.

Five of the acids listed in Table 13-1 are *polyprotic acids*, i.e., acids with more than one acidic H. For example, phosphoric acid ionizes in three steps:

$$PO(OH)_3(aq) + H_2O(l) \rightleftarrows H_3O^+(aq) + PO_2(OH)_2^-(aq) \quad pK_{a1} = 2.12$$

$$PO_2(OH)_2^-(aq) + H_2O(l) \rightleftarrows H_3O^+(aq) + PO_3(OH)^{2-}(aq) \quad pK_{a2} = 7.21$$

$$PO_3(OH)^{2-}(aq) + H_2O(l) \rightleftarrows H_3O^+(aq) + PO_4^{3-}(aq) \quad pK_{a3} = 12.67$$

Important Information

Strengths of oxoacids, $XO_n(OH)_m$
- $n = 3$: very strong acid, $pK_a \approx$ $(-7) - (-8)$;
- $n = 2$: strong acid, $pK_a \approx (-1) -$ (-3);
- $n = 1$: weak acid, $pK_a \approx 2\text{-}5$;
- $n = 0$: very weak acid, $pK_a \approx 7\text{-}$ 10.

The acidity of the neutral acid is in the range expected for an oxoacid with one oxo O. In the second and third steps, phosphoric acid is a much weaker acid. In general, we find that pK_a increases by about 5 for each successive ionization step for a polyprotic acid. An exception to this rule is oxalic acid, $H_2C_2O_4 = \text{HOOC-COOH}$, where the acidic -OH groups are bound to different C atoms and behave more nearly independently.

Acid-Base Equilibrium

A wide variety of problems are encountered based on acid-base equilibria. In this section, we examine three of the most common.

Note!

No all-purpose rules can be given for acid-base equilibrium problems. Skill increases with experience!

Calculation of pH of a solution of an acid or base. In performing a calculation based on an acid or base ionization constant expression such as Eqs. (13-7) or (13-8), there are often many unknowns. Remember that in an algebraic problem involving multiple unknowns, one needs as many equations as there are unknowns. The equilibrium constant expression itself is one equation, and the K_w expression is always available. Two other types of equation are often useful: equations expressing conservation of atoms or groups of atoms, and an equation expressing the charge neutrality of the solution.

Example 1. Compute the pH and the concentrations of the various species present in a 0.10 M solution of formic acid, HCOOH.

The species present in this solution are HCOOH, HCO_2^-, H_3O^+, and OH^-. With four unknowns, we need four equations:

Equilibrium constant expressions:

$$K_a = \frac{[H_3O^+][HCO_2^-]}{[HCOOH]} = 10^{-3.75} = 1.77 \times 10^{-4} \tag{i}$$

$$K_w = [H_3O^+][OH^-] = 1.00 \times 10^{-14} \tag{ii}$$

Conservation of formate:

$$[HCOOH] + [HCO_2^-] = 0.10 \text{ M} \tag{iii}$$

Conservation of charge:

$$[H_3O^+] = [HCO_2^-] + [OH^-] \tag{iv}$$

We expect the solution to be at least weakly acidic, which suggests that $[OH^-] \ll [H_3O^+]$ so that we can ignore $[OH^-]$ in Eq. (iv). Equations (iv) and (iii) give $[H_3O^+] = [HCO_2^-] = x$ and $[HCOOH] = 0.10 - x$. We can

	[HCOOH]	[HCO$_2^-$]	[H$_3$O$^+$]
initial	0.10	0	0
change	$-x$	$+x$	$+x$
equilibrium	$0.10 - x$	x	x

now set up a table, as in the equilibrium problems of Chapter 12:

Substituting into the equilibrium constant expression,

$$\frac{x^2}{0.10 - x} = 1.77 \times 10^{-4}$$

Solving the quadratic equation gives $x = 4.12 \times 10^{-3}$ or -4.30×10^{-3}. The negative root makes no sense and we conclude that $[H_3O^+] = [HCO_2^-]$ $= 4.12 \times 10^{-3}$ M, $[HCOOH] = 0.096$ M, pH = 2.38. Equation (ii) then gives $[OH^-] = 2.43 \times 10^{-12}$ M. Here x is not quite small enough to ignore compared with 0.10, but in other problems where K_a is smaller, it may be a reasonable approximation.

Example 2. What are the concentrations of $H_2C_2O_4$, $HC_2O_4^-$, and $C_2O_4^{2-}$ in a 0.015 M solution of oxalic acid with the pH adjusted to 4.00?

When the pH is known, it is most convenient to use the logarithmic forms of the equilibrium constant expressions,

$$4.00 = 1.23 + \log \frac{[HC_2O_4^-]}{[H_2C_2O_4]} = 4.19 + \log \frac{[C_2O_4^{2-}]}{[HC_2O_4^-]}$$

From these, we can compute the concentration ratios,

$$[HC_2O_4^-] = 589 \, [H_2C_2O_4] \quad [C_2O_4^{2-}] = 0.646 \, [HC_2O_4^-]$$

or

$$[C_2O_4^{2-}] = 380 \, [H_2C_2O_4]$$

Since

$$[H_2C_2O_4] + [HC_2O_4^-] + [C_2O_4^{2-}] = 0.015 \text{ M}$$

we have

$$[H_2C_2O_4] (1 + 589 + 380) = 0.0155$$

Thus $[H_2C_2O_4] = 1.55 \times 10^{-5}$, $[HC_2O_4^-] = 9.1 \times 10^{-3}$, and $[C_2O_4^{2-}] = 5.9 \times 10^{-3}$ M.

pH titration curves. Acid solutions are often analyzed by titration with a solution of a strong base of known concentration; similarly, solutions of bases are analyzed by titration with a strong acid. In either case, the measured pH is plotted as a function of the titrant volume. Calculation of a pH titration curve is a particularly good introduction to acid-base equilibrium calculations since a variety of calculations are involved.

Example 3. Compute the pH vs. volume curve for the titration of 10.0 mL of 0.25 M HCl with 0.10 M NaOH.

Since HCl and NaOH are completely dissociated in dilute solutions, and the reaction goes to completion, this is really a simple stoichiometry problem in which we convert the H_3O^+ concentration to pH. If the initial number of millimoles of HCl is

$$n_0 = (0.25 \text{ mmol/mL})(10 \text{ mL}) = 2.5 \text{ mmol}$$

then, before complete neutralization $[H_3O^+]$ after the addition of V mL of NaOH solution is

$$[H_3O^+] = \frac{n_0 - V_{NaOH} C_{NaOH}}{V_{total}} = \frac{2.5 - 0.10 \, V_{NaOH}}{V_{NaOH} + 10}$$

We set up a table for several volumes of NaOH added:

V_{NaOH}	$[H_3O^+]$	pH	V_{NaOH}	$[H_3O^+]$	pH
0.00	0.250	0.60	15.00	0.040	1.40
5.00	0.133	0.88	20.00	0.0167	1.78
10.00	0.075	1.12	24.90	0.000286	3.54

When we add exactly 25.00 mL of NaOH, all the H_3O^+ from the HCl has been consumed—the *equivalence point*. The solution then contains NaCl, and, since Na^+ and Cl^- are neither acidic or basic, the H_3O^+ concentration is due to water ionization alone and pH = 7.00. Beyond the equivalence point, the solution will contain excess OH^-, the concentration of which is

$$[OH^-] = \frac{V_{NaOH} C_{NaOH} - n_0}{V_{total}} = \frac{0.10 V_{NaOH} - 2.5}{V_{NaOH} + 10}$$

and the pH is computed as pH = 14.00 – log[OH^-]. Continuing the table for two more points:

V_{NaOH}	$[OH^-]$	pH	V_{NaOH}	$[OH^-]$	pH
25.10	0.00029	10.46	30.00	0.0125	12.10

These points (and a few more) are plotted in Figure 13-2.

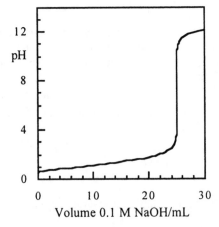

Figure 13-2. pH titration curve for titration of 10 mL of 0.25 M HCl with 0.10 M NaOH.

Example 4. Compute the pH vs. V curve for the titration of 20.0 mL of 0.15 M acetic acid, CH_3COOH, with 0.10 M NaOH.

With a weak acid, the calculations are a bit more complex. We begin by computing the initial pH, using the method of Example 1, pH = 2.79. At the equivalence point, we have 50.0 mL of 0.060 M sodium acetate. Since acetate is the base conjugate to a weak acid, the solution is basic and we must compute the pH. From eq (13-12) for acetate ion, $K_b = K_w/K_a = 5.62 \times 10^{-10}$, and the equilibrium constant expression is

$$K_b = \frac{[CH_3COOH][OH^-]}{[CH_3CO_2^-]} = \frac{x^2}{0.060 - x} = 5.62 \times 10^{-10}$$

We find $x = [OH^-] = 5.81 \times 10^{-6}$ M, pOH = 5.24, pH = 8.76. Note that the pH at the equivalence point is *not* 7.00—the solution is weakly basic. Points between $V = 0$ and $V = 30$ mL are most easily computed by noting that OH^- reacts with CH_3COOH to produce $CH_3CO_2^-$. For example, when 5.00 mL of NaOH is added, the concentrations are

$$[CH_3CO_2^-] = \frac{(5.0 \text{ mL})(0.10 \text{ mmol/mL})}{25.0 \text{ mL}} = 0.020 \text{ M}$$

$$[CH_3COOH] = \frac{3.0 \text{ mmol} - 0.50 \text{ mmol}}{25.0 \text{ mL}} = 0.10 \text{ M}$$

Substituting in Eq. (13-10), we have

$$pH = 4.75 + \log \frac{0.020}{0.100} = 4.05$$

Beyond the equivalence point, we compute the pH as in Example 3. The complete titration curve is shown in Figure 13-3.

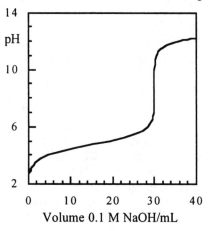

Figure 13-3. pH titration curve for titration of 20 mL of 0.15 M CH_3COOH with 0.10 M NaOH.

Notice that, according to Eq. (13-10), when $[CH_3COOH] = [CH_3CO_2^-]$, $pH = pK_a$. The two concentrations are equal when exactly half the CH_3COOH has been converted to $CH_3CO_2^-$, i.e., half-way to the equivalence point. In titration curves for weak acids, the pH at the *half-equivalence point* is usually equal to pK_a. (This generalization fails when concentrations are very small or the acid insufficiently weak.)

Buffer Solutions. In Figure 13-3, we see that the pH changes most slowly in the vicinity of the half-equivalence point, the *buffer region*. Small additions of base (or acid) to a solution containing comparable amounts of an acid and its conjugate base change the pH only slightly; the solution is said to be *buffered* against pH changes.

Consider 100 mL of a solution containing 0.1 M CH_3COOH and 0.1 M $CH_3CO_2^-$, $pH = 4.75$. Addition of 10^{-3} mol of HCl would change the ratio $[CH_3CO_2^-]/[CH_3COOH]$ from 0.1/0.1 to 0.09/0.11 and the pH would change from 4.75 to 4.66. We could, of course, prepare 100 mL of a pH 4.75 solution by diluting HCl to 1.78×10^{-5} M. However, addition of 10^{-3} mol of HCl would reduce the pH to 2.0, a much bigger change than for the buffer solution.

Example 5. How many moles of NaH_2PO_4 and Na_2HPO_4 should be used to prepare 250 mL of a solution with a total phosphate concentration of 0.10 M and pH = 7.00?

The relevant equilibrium is the second proton transfer step for phosphoric acid,

$$H_2PO_4^-(aq) + H_2O(l) \rightleftarrows H_3O^+(aq) + HPO_4^{2-}(aq) \qquad pK_a = 7.21$$

$$pH = 7.00 = 7.21 + \log \frac{[HPO_4^{2-}]}{[H_2PO_4^-]} \qquad \frac{[HPO_4^{2-}]}{[H_2PO_4^-]} = 0.617$$

Since $\qquad [H_2PO_4^-] + [HPO_4^{2-}] = 0.10$ M

we have $\qquad [H_2PO_4^-] = 0.062$ M, $[HPO_4^{2-}] = 0.038$ M

and to prepare 250 mL of solution, we need 0.0154 mol of NaH_2PO_4 and 0.0095 mol of Na_2HPO_4.

Problems

13.1 Write the formulas for the conjugate bases of the following acids: (a) HCN, (b) HCO_3^-, (c) $N_2H_5^+$, (d) CH_3CH_2OH
 Ans. (a) CN^-, (b) CO_3^{2-}, (c) N_2H_4, (d) $CH_3CH_2O^-$
13.2 Write the formulas for the conjugate acids of the following bases: (a) CH_3COOH, (b) HCO_3^-, (c) C_5H_5N, (d) $N_2H_5^+$.
 Ans. (a) $CH_3C(OH)_2^+$, (b) H_2CO_3, (c) $C_5H_5NH^+$, (d) $N_2H_6^{2+}$

13.3 Consider the reaction, $CO_2(g) + OH^-(aq) \rightarrow HCO_3^-(aq)$. According to which set of definitions is this an acid-base reaction? Which is the acid? *Ans.* CO_2 acts as a Lewis acid

13.4 ΔH^0 for the ionization of water (eq. (13-3)) is 55.90 kJ. Calculate K_w at 37°C. What is the pH of pure water at 37°C?
Ans. 2.4×10^{-14}, pH = 6.81

13.5 What are the concentrations of (a) H_3PO_4 and (b) PO_4^{3-} in the buffer solution of Example 5?
Ans. (a) 8.1×10^{-7}, (b) 8.2×10^{-8} M

13.6 Calculate the molar concentration at which an acetic acid solution is 2.0% ionized. *Ans.* 0.043 M

13.7 A solution contains 0.0100 M chloroacetic acid, $ClCH_2COOH$, $K_a = 1.40 \times 10^{-3}$, and 0.0020 M sodium chloroacetate. What is the pH? *Ans.* pH = 2.62

13.8 Calculate the concentrations of H_3O^+, CH_3COOH, and $CH_3CO_2^-$ in a solution containing 0.100 M acetic acid and 0.050 M HCl. *Ans.* 0.050, 0.100, 3.5×10^{-5} M, respectively

13.9 Calculate the pH and pOH of a 0.0100 M solution of NH_3.
Ans. pH = 10.62, pOH = 3.38

13.10 Calculate the pH and pOH of a 0.0100 M solution of NH_4Cl.
Ans. pH = 5.63, pOH = 8.37

13.11 25.0 mL of 0.10 M HClO is titrated with 0.10 M NaOH. Compute the pH when (a) 0, (b) 6.25, (c) 12.5, (d) 18.75, and (e) 25.00 mL of NaOH solution has been added.
Ans. (a) 4.26, (b) 7.05, (c) 7.53, (d) 8.01, (e) 10.11

13.12 The base imidazole, $K_b = 1.11 \times 10^{-7}$, is to be used to prepare a solution buffered to pH 7.00. What volumes of 0.0200 M HCl and 0.0200 M imiazole should be mixed to prepare 100 mL of buffer solution? *Ans.* 65.5 mL base, 34.5 ml acid

13.13 The pH titration curve for the titration of 25 mL of a solution of CH_3NH_2 with 0.10 M HCl is shown. What is the approximate pK_a of $CH_3NH_3^+$? the pK_b of CH_3NH_2?
Ans. 0.075 M, pK_a = 10.6, pK_b = 3.4

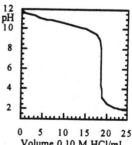

Chapter 14

PRECIPITATES AND COMPLEX IONS

IN THIS CHAPTER:

✔ *Solubility Equilibrium*
✔ *Complexation Equilibria*

Solubility Equilibrium

Consider the equilibrium between solid silver chloride and Ag^+ and Cl^- in a saturated aqueous solution:

$$AgCl(s) \rightleftarrows Ag^+(aq) + Cl^-(aq)$$

The equilibrium constant expression is

$$K_{sp} = [Ag^+][Cl^-] = 1.6 \times 10^{-10}$$

Solid AgCl does not appear in the equilibrium constant expression since it is presumed to be pure solid and thus in its standard state. The subscript *sp* designates K as a *solubility-product constant*.

You Need to Know

The solubility-product equilibrium constant for a weakly soluble salt, M_nA_m, is: $K_{sp} = [M^{z+}]^n[A^{z-}]^m$.

The solubility product constant allows us to predict the degree of completeness of precipitation reactions. Whenever the product of the concentrations (each raised to the appropriate power) exceeds K_{sp}, the salt will precipitate until the concentration product equals K_{sp}.

Example 1. Compute the solubility of $Pb(IO_3)_2$ in pure water,

$$Pb(IO_3)_2(s) \rightleftarrows Pb^{2+}(aq) + 2 IO_3^-(aq)$$

$$K_{sp} = [Pb^{2+}][IO_3^-]^2 = 2.5 \times 10^{-13}$$

Set up a table as in Chapters 12 and 13:

	$[Pb^{2+}]$/M	$[IO_3^-]$/M
initial	0	0
equilibrium	x	$2x$

$$x\,(2x)^2 = 4\,x^3 = 2.5 \times 10^{-13}$$

from which we find $x = [Pb^{2+}] = 4.0 \times 10^{-5}$ M, $[IO_3^-] = 8.0 \times 10^{-5}$ M. The solubility of $Pb(IO_3)_2$ thus is 4.0×10^{-5} mol/L.

Example 2. Compute the solubility of $Pb(IO_3)_2$ in 0.10 M $NaIO_3$.

	$[Pb^{2+}]$/M	$[IO_3^-]$/M
initial	0	0.10
equilibrium	x	$0.10 + 2x$

Substituting into the equilibrium constant expression, we have

$$(x)(0.10 + 2x)^2 = 2.5 \times 10^{-13}$$

On expansion, this will lead to a cubic equation in x. We could go ahead and solve the cubic equation, but there is an easier way. We realize that x is going to be small, probably small enough that $2x$ is negligible compared with 0.10. Making that approximation, we have

$$0.010\,x = 2.5 \times 10^{-13}$$

$x = [Pb^{2+}] = 2.5 \times 10^{-11}$, the solubility of $Pb(IO_3)_2$ in 0.10 M $NaIO_3$.

Example 3. Solid NaF is added in tiny increments to a solution containing 0.10 M $CaCl_2$ and 0.10 M $MgCl_2$. CaF_2 and MgF_2 are rather insoluble with

$$[Ca^{2+}][F^-]^2 = 3.9 \times 10^{-11} \quad [Mg^{2+}][F^-]^2 = 6.6 \times 10^{-9}$$

Which salt—CaF_2 or MgF_2—precipitates first? When the first trace of the second precipitate appears, what are the concentrations of Ca^{2+} and Mg^{2+}?

The salt with the smaller value of K_{sp} will precipitate first, CaF_2. When the first trace of MgF_2 precipitates, we can assume that $[Mg^{2+}]$ is still approximately 0.10 M, so that $[F^-]$ must satisfy the equilibrium constant expression

$$(0.10 \text{ M}) [F^-]^2 = 6.6 \times 10^{-9}$$

$[F^-] = 2.6 \times 10^{-4}$ M. Substituting this in the K_{sp} expression for CaF_2,

$$[Ca^{2+}](2.6 \times 10^{-4})^2 = 3.9 \times 10^{-11}$$

and $[Ca^{2+}] = 5.9 \times 10^{-4}$ M. The percentage of Ca^{2+} remaining in solution is $5.9 \times 10^{-4} \times 100/0.10$, or 0.6%. Thus 99.4% of the Ca^{2+} has been removed from solution.

Example 3 demonstrates one application of solubility equilibria: precipitation can be used to selectively remove one component of a solution, i.e., the Mg^{2+} and Ca^{2+} can be separated.

The solubility of a precipitate can be decreased by addition of one of the product ions, as demonstrated by Example 2. The solubility can be increased by removal of one of the product ions. If the anion is a base, it can be consumed by addition of strong acid. For example, $Mg(OH)_2$ is insoluble, $K_{sp} = 1.2 \times 10^{-11}$, but if enough HCl is added, the OH^- ions are consumed and $Mg(OH)_2$ goes into solution,

$$Mg(OH)_2(s) + 2 H_3O^+(aq) \rightarrow Mg^{2+}(aq) + 4 H_2O(l)$$

Example 4. Compute the solubility of MgF_2 in pure water and in a solution buffered at pH 2.00. The pK_a of HF is 3.45.

In pure water, we have $[Mg^{2+}] = 0.5 [F^-]$; substituting into the K_{sp} expression,

$$K_{sp} = 6.6 \times 10^{-9} = [Mg^{2+}][F^-]^2 = 0.5 [F^-]^3$$

and $[F^-] = 2.4 \times 10^{-3}$, $[Mg^{2+}] = 1.2 \times 10^{-3}$ M. At pH 2.00, the logarithmic form of the HF/F^- equilibrium constant expression gives

$$pH = 2.00 = 3.45 + \log \frac{[F^-]}{[HF]}$$

Thus $[HF] = 28 [F^-]$, and

$$[Mg^{2+}] = 0.5 [F^-]_{total} = 0.5 ([F^-] + [HF]) = 0.5 \times 29 [F^-]$$

Substituting into the K_{sp} expression, we have

$$6.6 \times 10^{-9} = 14.5 [F^-]^3$$

$[F^-] = 7.7 \times 10^{-4}$, $[Mg^{2+}] = 0.011$ M, about 10 times greater than the solubility in pure water.

Complexation Equilibria

Metal ions such as Cu^{2+} are Lewis acids that combine with Lewis bases such as H_2O to form *complex ions*, e.g., $Cu(OH_2)_4^{2+}$. The number of ligands, the *coordination number*, varies from one metal ion to another; the most common coordination numbers are 4 and 6, but 2, 3, 5, 7, and 8 are also known. In the presence of another Lewis base such as NH_3, the H_2O ligands can be replaced in stepwise equilibria:

$$Cu(OH_2)_4^{2+} + NH_3 \rightleftarrows Cu(OH_2)_3(NH_3)^{2+} + H_2O$$

$$Cu(OH_2)_3(NH_3)^{2+} + NH_3 \rightleftarrows Cu(OH_2)_2(NH_3)_2^{2+} + H_2O$$

$$Cu(OH_2)_2(NH_3)_2^{2+} + NH_3 \rightleftarrows Cu(OH_2)(NH_3)_3^{2+} + H_2O$$

$$Cu(OH_2)_3(NH_3)^{2+} + NH_3 \rightleftarrows Cu(NH_3)_4^{2+} + H_2O$$

$$K_n = \frac{[Cu(OH_2)_{4-n}(NH_3)_n^{2+}]}{[Cu(OH_2)_{5-n}(NH_3)_{n-1}^{2+}][NH_3]}$$

$K_1 = 1.6 \times 10^4$, $K_2 = 3.2 \times 10^3$, $K_2 = 9.5 \times 10^2$, $K_4 = 1.3 \times 10^2$. Since $\Delta H°$ is nearly the same for each step, -23 kJ/mol, the decrease of K_n with increasing NH_3 substitution is an entropy effect which can be partly explained by statistics. In the first step, any one of four H_2O ligands can be replaced in the forward reaction but only one NH_3 can be replaced in the reverse reaction, contributing a factor of 4 to K_1. In the fourth step, the statistics are reversed, one H_2O can be replaced in the forward reaction but any of four NH_3 ligands can be replaced in the reverse step, contributing a factor of 1/4 to K_4.

We sometimes can use the overall formation constant corresponding to the sum of the four steps,

$$Cu(OH_2)_4^{2+} + 4 NH_3 \rightleftarrows Cu(NH_3)_4^{2+} + 4 H_2O$$

$$K_f = \frac{[Cu(NH_3)_4^{2+}]}{[Cu(OH_2)_4^{2+}][NH_3]^4} = K_1 K_2 K_3 K_4 = 6 \times 10^{12}$$

Example 5. Compute the concentration of $Cu(OH_2)_4^{2+}$ in a solution with a total Cu^{2+} and NH_3 concentrations of 0.10 and 1.0 M, respectively.

The formation of $Cu(NH_3)_4^{2+}$ is nearly complete since K_f is so large. Thus to a good approximation, $[Cu(NH_3)_4^{2+}] = 0.10$ M, $[NH_3] = 0.6$ M. Substitution into the equilibrium constant expression gives $[Cu(OH_2)_4^{2+}] = 1.3 \times 10^{-13}$ M.

Complexation equilibria involve replacement of ligands surrounding a metal ion by other Lewis bases, e.g.,

$$Ag(OH_2)_2^+ + 2\ NH_3 \rightleftarrows Ag(NH_3)_2^+ + 2\ H_2O$$

$$K_f = \frac{[Ag(NH_3)_2^+]}{[Ag(OH_2)_2^+][NH_3]^2}$$

Bidentate ligands such as ethylene diamine, $NH_2CH_2CH_2NH_2$ (en), form *chelate* complexes with metals ions such as Cu^{2+}. The term *chelate* is derived from the Greek word for "claw" and is intended to invoke the image of the "two-toothed" ligand "biting" the metal. The two steps of the equilibrium are:

$$Cu(OH_2)_4^{2+} + en \rightleftarrows Cu(OH_2)_2(en)^{2+} + 2\ H_2O$$

$$Cu(OH_2)_2(en)^{2+} + en \rightleftarrows Cu(en)_2^{2+} + 2\ H_2O$$

$$K_n = \frac{[Cu(OH_2)_{4-2n}(en)_n^{2+}]}{[Cu(OH_2)_{6-2n}(en)_{n-1}^{2+}][en]}$$

where $K_1 = 4.9 \times 10^{10}$, $K_2 = 1.3 \times 10^9$. Although $\Delta H°$ for each step is approximately equal to twice $\Delta H°$ for the NH_3 complexation steps—2 Cu-O bonds broken, 2 Cu-N bonds formed—the equilibrium constants are much larger than would have been expected from the NH_3 equilibria—$K_1K_2 = 5 \times 10^7$ and $K_3K_4 = 1 \times 10^5$. This effect is due to the additional entropy produced when two H_2O molecules are released but only one en is removed from solution. Similar enhancement of the complex formation equilibrium constant—the *chelate effect*—is observed when a bidentate ligand replaces two monodentate ligands.

When the metal ion of an insoluble salt forms a complex ion, the aquo cation is removed from solution, shifting the solubility equilibrium toward solution species.

Example 6. What is the solubility of AgSCN ($K_{sp} = 1.1 \times 10^{-12}$) in pure water and in 0.010 M NH_3? Ag^+ forms an NH_3 complex,

> The formation of *chelate* complexes with one *bidentate* ligand replacing two *monodentate* ligands is enhanced by the entropy increase when the number of molecules increases.

Note!

$$Ag(OH_2)_2^+ + 2\,NH_3 \rightleftarrows Ag(NH_3)_2^+ + 2\,H_2O$$

$$K_f = \frac{[Ag(NH_3)_2^+]}{[Ag(OH_2)_2^+][NH_3]^2} = 1.7 \times 10^7$$

In pure water, $[Ag^+] = [SCN^-]$ and the K_{sp} expression gives
$$K_{sp} = 1.1 \times 10^{-12} = [Ag^+][SCN^-] = [Ag^+]^2$$
so the $[Ag^+] = [SCN^-] = 1.05 \times 10^{-6}$ M.

Assume that insufficient $Ag(NH_3)_2^+$ is formed to significantly diminish the NH_3 concentration from 0.010 M. Substituting into the K_f expression leads to $[Ag(NH_3)_2^+] = 1.7 \times 10^3\,[Ag^+]$.

Thus $\quad [SCN^-] = [Ag^+] + [Ag(NH_3)_2^+] = 1.7 \times 10^3\,[Ag^+]$

$$1.1 \times 10^{-12} = [Ag^+][SCN^-] = 1.7 \times 10^3\,[Ag^+]^2$$

$[Ag^+] = 2.5 \times 10^{-8}$ M, $[Ag(NH_3)_2^+] = [SCN^-] = 4.3 \times 10^{-5}$ M. Note that $[NH_3] = 0.010 - 2(4.3 \times 10^{-5}) = 0.0099$ M, almost unchanged, thus validating our assumption.

Problems

14.1 The solubility of $PbSO_4$ in water is 0.038 g/L. Calculate K_{sp}.
Ans. 1.6×10^{-8}

14.2 Calculate the solubility of CaF_2 ($K_{sp} = 3.9 \times 10^{-11}$) in 0.015 M NaF solution. *Ans.* 1.7×10^{-7} M

14.3 Calculate the concentrations of Ag^+, CrO_4^{2-}, NO_3^-, and K^+ after 30 mL of 0.010 M $AgNO_3$ is mixed with 20 mL of 0.010 M K_2CrO_4. K_{sp} for Ag_2CrO_4 is 1.9×10^{-12}.
Ans. $[Ag^+] = 4.3 \times 10^{-5}$ M, $[CrO_4^{2-}] = 0.00102$ M,
$[NO_3^-] = 0.0060$ M, $[K^+] = 0.0080$ M

14.4 A solution contains 0.00100 M $MgCl_2$. (a) Calculate the maximum concentration of OH^- without precipitating $Mg(OH)_2$, K_{sp} = 7.1 × 10^{-12}. If the solution also has $[NH_3]$ = 0.0100 M, what concentration of NH_4Cl must be present to avoid precipitation of $Mg(OH)_2$?
Ans. (a) 8.4 × 10^{-5} M, (b) 0.0021 M

14.5 Calculate the simultaneous solubilities of CaF_2 (K_{sp} = 3.9 × 10^{-11}) and BaF_2 (K_{sp} = 1.7 × 10^{-6}) in pure water.
Ans. $[Ca^{2+}]$ = 1.7 × 10^{-7}, $[Ba^{2+}]$ = 7.5 × 10^{-3} M

14.6 Calculate the simultaneous solubilities of AgBr (K_{sp} = 7.7 × 10^{-13}) and AgSCN (K_{sp} = 1.1 × 10^{-12}) in pure water.
Ans. [AgBr] = 5.6 × 10^{-7} M, [AgSCN] = 8.0 × 10^{-7} M

14.7 500 mL of 0.0100 M $AgNO_3$ is mixed with 500 mL of a solution 0.0100 M in NaCl and 0.0100 M in NaBr. Calculate $[Ag^+]$, $[Cl^-]$, and $[Br^-]$. K_{sp} (AgCl) = 1.6 × 10^{-10}, K_{sp} (AgBr) = 7.7 × 10^{-13}.
Ans. $[Ag^+]$ = 3.4 × 10^{-8}, $[Cl^-]$ = 4.8 × 10^{-3}, $[Br^-]$ = 2.3 × 10^{-5} M

14.8 Equal volumes of 0.0100 M $Sr(NO_3)_2$ and 0.0100 M $NaHSO_4$ are mixed. Calculate $[Sr^{2+}]$ and $[H_3O^+]$. K_{sp} = 3.2 × 10^{-7} for $SrSO_4$ and K_{a2} = 0.012 for H_2SO_4. *Hint:* No species is of negligible concentration; use conservation and charge balance relations in addition to equilibrium constant expressions.
Ans. $[Sr^{2+}]$ = 6.7 × 10^{-4}, $[H_3O^+]$ = 4.8 × 10^{-3} M

14.9 Silver ion forms $Ag(CN)_2^-$ in the presence of excess CN^-, K_f = 3.0 × 10^{20}. How much KCN should be added to 1 L of a 0.00050 M $AgNO_3$ solution in order to reduce $[Ag^+]$ to 1.0 × 10^{-19} M?
Ans. 0.0051 mol

14.10 How much NH_3 must be added to a solution containing 0.0040 M Ag^+ and 0.0010 M Cl^- to avoid precipitation of AgCl, K_{sp} = 1.6 × 10^{-10}. K_f for $Ag(NH_3)_2^+$ is 1.67 × 10^7.
Ans. $[NH_3]_{free}$ = 0.039 M, $[NH_3]_{total}$ = 0.047 M

14.11 The formation constants for $Fe(OH_3)_{6-n}(SCN)_n^{3-n}$ are K_1 = 130, K_2 = 16, and K_3 = 1.0. Compute the concentrations of Fe^{3+}, $FeSCN^{2+}$, $Fe(SCN)_2^+$, and $Fe(SCN)_3$ in a solution with $[Fe]_{total}$ = 0.010 M and $[SCN^-]_{free}$ = 0.050 M.
Ans. $[Fe^{3+}]$ = 7.7 × 10^{-4}, $[FeSCN^{2+}]$ = 5.0 × 10^{-3}, $[Fe(SCN)_2^+]$ = 4.0 × 10^{-3}, $[Fe(SCN)_3]$ = 2.0 × 10^{-4} M

Chapter 15
ELECTRO-
CHEMISTRY

IN THIS CHAPTER:

✔ Faraday's Laws of Electrolysis
✔ Galvanic Cells and Standard Half-
   Cell Potentials
✔ Concentration Cells and the
   Glass Electrode

Introduction

In this chapter, we will deal with experiments that measure electric potentials and currents. Electric potential is measured in volts (V), electric charge in coulombs (C), and electric current in amperes (1 A = 1 C/s). Electrical work is done when a charge Q is passed through a potential difference, ΔV, with 1 J = 1 V•C,

$$w = Q\,\Delta V \qquad (15\text{-}1)$$

Faraday's Laws of Electrolysis

Chemists began passing electric current through solutions in the early 19th century; early results included the isolation of most of the alkali and alkaline earth metals by Humphry Davy. Davy's assistant, Michael Faraday, went on to study the quantitative aspects of electrolysis. By the 1830s, Faraday had accumulated enough data to summarize his findings in two laws: (1) The mass of a substance liberated at or deposited on an electrode is proportional to the electric charge passed through the electrolyte. (2) The mass of such a substance is proportional to the molar mass of the substance, adjusted for the number of electrons required for the oxidation or reduction process. (Faraday's work was 40 years before the discovery of the electron so he worded the second law somewhat differently.)

The charge on 1 mol of electrons is the Faraday constant, $1F = 96485$ C/mol. When current is passed through a solution of $CuSO_4$, Cu^{2+} is reduced at the *cathode* and water is oxidized at the *anode*:

$$2\ Cu^{2+}(aq) + 4\ e^- \rightarrow 2\ Cu(s)$$

$$2\ H_2O(l) \rightarrow O_2(g) + 4\ H^+(aq) + 4\ e^-$$

If $1.000F$ of charge is passed through the solution, 29.5g (0.500 mol) of metallic copper is deposited on the cathode and 8.00 g (0.250 mol) of $O_2(g)$ is liberated at the anode. In general, reduction occurs at the cathode and oxidation at the anode.

Faraday's laws can be summarized by:

- 1 faraday (F) = 96,485 C/mol electrons;
- Mole relationships apply to electrons in balanced oxidation-reduction half-reactions.

Galvanic Cells and Standard Half-Cell Potentials

Here we investigate some of the properties of galvanic cells, cells used to produce an electric potential. Luigi Galvani discovered the first such cell by accident in 1791. Following Galvani's discovery, Alessandro Volta developed a practical cell in 1800, and it was Volta's cell that led to the work of Davy and Faraday.

Consider the electrochemical cell shown in Figure 15-1. Pieces of zinc and copper are immersed, respectively, in solutions of $ZnSO_4$ and $CuSO_4$. The solutions are in contact through a glass frit which is sufficiently porous to allow ions to pass through, but which will prevent mixing of the solutions. When a voltmeter is attached between the Zn and Cu electrodes, it is found that an electric potential has developed.

If the voltmeter is replaced by a resistor and an ammeter, it is found that an electric current flows. If, after current has flowed for some time, the electrodes are removed and weighed, it is found that the Zn electrode has lost mass and the Cu electrode has gained mass. The electrode mass changes are as expected from Faraday's laws if the processes at the Zn and Cu electrodes are the half-reactions:

$$Zn(s) \rightarrow Zn^{2+}(aq) + 2\ e^-$$
$$Cu^{2+}(aq) + 2\ e^- \rightarrow Cu(s)$$

The overall cell reaction,

$$Cu^{2+}(aq) + Zn(s) \rightarrow Cu(s) + Zn^{2+}(aq)$$

is a spontaneous process, $\Delta G° = -212.8$ kJ, and it is this spontaneous process which leads to the electric potential.

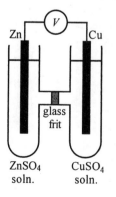

ZnSO₄ soln. CuSO₄ soln.

Figure 15-1. A galvanic cell.

An electrochemical cell generates a potential difference E. (The symbol E, commonly used in electrochemistry, refers to *electromotive force*, an archaic term for potential difference.) The electrical work done when n moles of electrons is passed by the cell can be found using Eq. (15-1), $w = -nFE$. It can be shown that the electrical work done by an electrochemical cell, at constant temperature and pressure, is equal to the change in Gibbs free energy of the cell components,

$$\Delta G = -nFE \tag{15-2}$$

If the cell reaction is spontaneous, $\Delta G < 0$ and $E > 0$, hence the negative sign in Eq. (15-2). Combining Eqs. (15-2) and (12-10), we have the *Nernst equation*, which relates E to the reaction quotient Q:

$$\Delta G = \Delta G° + RT \ln Q \tag{12-10}$$

$$-nFE = -nFE° + RT \ln Q$$

$$E = E° - \frac{RT}{nF} \ln Q \tag{15-3}$$

where $E° = -\Delta G°/nF$ is the *standard potential* of the cell, i.e., the potential of the cell when all species are in standard states. We sometimes use the Nernst equation with $T = 298$ K and the natural logarithm converted to base 10:

$$E = E° - \frac{0.0592}{n} \log Q \tag{15-4}$$

Example 1. Compute the potential of the cell shown in Figure 15-1 when $T = 298$ K, $[Cu^{2+}] = 0.010$ M, $[Zn^{2+}] = 0.0050$ M.

The standard potential is computed from $\Delta G°$,

Essential Point

The key connection between an electrochemical cell potential E and thermodynamics is:

$$\Delta G = -nFE$$

where n is the number of moles of electrons transferred in the cell reaction for which ΔG is the change in Gibbs free energy.

$$E° = \frac{\Delta G°}{nF} = -\frac{-212.8 \times 10^3 \text{ J}}{(2 \text{ mol})(96485 \text{ C/mol})} = 1.103 \text{ V}$$

$$E = 1.103 - \frac{0.0592}{2} \log\frac{[Zn^{2+}]}{[Cu^{2+}]} = 1.103 - 0.0296 \log\frac{0.0050}{0.010} = 1.112 \text{ V}$$

An electrochemical cell reaction, like any oxidation-reduction reaction, can be written as the sum of an oxidation half-reaction and a reduction half-reaction. In the case of a cell, these half-reactions correspond to the reactions at the two electrodes. Since the cell reaction is the sum of the half-cell reactions, it is convenient to think of dividing the cell potential into half-cell potentials. Unfortunately, there is no way of measuring a half-cell potential—we always need two half-cells to make a cell, the potential of which is measurable. By convention, the half-cell reaction,

$$2 \text{ H}^+(\text{aq}) + 2 \text{ e}^- \rightarrow \text{H}_2(\text{g}) \tag{15-5}$$

has been chosen as the primary reference half-cell with standard potential taken to be $E° = 0.000$ V. *Standard half-cell potentials* then are determined by cells that include Eq. (15-5) as one of the half-cell reactions. Thus the standard potential of the cell with cell reaction

$$2 \text{ H}^+(\text{aq}) + \text{Zn}(\text{s}) \rightarrow \text{H}_2(\text{g}) + \text{Zn}^{2+}(\text{aq})$$

has
$$E°_{cell} = E°_{H^+/H_2} + E°_{Zn/Zn^{2+}} = E°_{Zn/Zn^{2+}}$$

where $E°_{Zn/Zn^{2+}}$ is the standard potential for the half-cell,

$$\text{Zn}(\text{s}) \rightarrow \text{Zn}^{2+}(\text{aq}) + 2 \text{ e}^-$$

Standard half-cell potentials are usually tabulated as reduction potentials, e.g.,

$$\text{Zn}^{2+}(\text{aq}) + 2 \text{ e}^- \rightarrow \text{Zn}(\text{s}) \qquad E° = -0.763 \text{ V}$$

The corresponding oxidation half-cell potential is the negative of this value, i.e., $E°_{Zn/Zn^{2+}} = +0.763$ V. Some standard reduction half-cell potentials are given in Table 15-1.

Standard half-cell potentials can be used to compute standard cell potentials, standard Gibbs free energy changes, and equilibrium constants for oxidation-reduction reactions.

Example 2. Compute (a) the standard potential for a cell with cell reaction.

$$\text{MnO}_4^- + 8 \text{ H}^+ + 5 \text{ Fe}^{2+} \rightarrow \text{Mn}^{2+} + 5 \text{ Fe}^{3+} + 4 \text{ H}_2\text{O}$$

(b) $\Delta G°$ for the reaction, and (c) the equilibrium constant K.

The cell reaction is the sum of the half-reactions:

reduction: $\text{MnO}_4^-(\text{aq}) + 8 \text{ H}^+(\text{aq}) + 5 \text{ e}^- \rightarrow \text{Mn}^{2+}(\text{aq}) + 4 \text{ H}_2\text{O}(\text{l})$
oxidation: $\qquad\qquad 5 \text{ Fe}^{2+}(\text{aq}) \rightarrow 5 \text{ Fe}^{3+}(\text{aq}) + 5 \text{ e}^-$

Given the standard free energy changes for the half-reactions, we have

$$\Delta G° = \Delta G°_{\text{reduction}} + \Delta G°_{\text{oxidation}}$$
$$\Delta G° = -5FE°_{\text{MnO}_4^-/\text{Mn}^{2+}} + 5FE°_{\text{Fe}^{3+}/\text{Fe}^{2+}} = -5FE°_{\text{cell}}$$
$$E°_{\text{cell}} = E°_{\text{MnO}_4^-/\text{Mn}^{2+}} - E°_{\text{Fe}^{3+}/\text{Fe}^{2+}}$$

(a) $$E°_{\text{cell}} = 1.51 - 0.77 = 0.74 \text{ V}$$

(b) $$\Delta G° = -(5 \text{ mol})(96485 \text{ C/mol})(0.74 \text{ V}) = -357 \times 10^3 \text{ J}$$

(c) $$K = e^{-\Delta G°/RT} = 4 \times 10^{62}$$

A general result is demonstrated by Example 2:

$$E°_{\text{cell}} = E°(\text{reduction half-cell}) - E°(\text{oxidation half-cell})$$

Table 15-1. Standard Reduction Half-Cell Potentials

Half-cell reaction	$E°$/V	Half-cell reaction	$E°$/V
$F_2(g) + 2 e^- \rightarrow 2 F^-(aq)$	2.87	$Li^+(aq) + e^- \rightarrow Li(s)$	−3.04
$Cl_2(g) + 2 e^- \rightarrow 2 Cl^-(aq)$	1.36	$Na^+(aq) + e^- \rightarrow Na(s)$	−2.71
$Br_2(l) + 2 e^- \rightarrow 2 Br^-(aq)$	1.06	$K^+(aq) + e^- \rightarrow K(s)$	−2.92
$I_2(s) + 2 e^- \rightarrow 2 I^-(aq)$	0.62	$Mg^{2+}(aq) + 2 e^- \rightarrow Mg(s)$	−2.36
$Ag^+(aq) + e^- \rightarrow Ag(s)$	0.80	$Ca^{2+}(aq) + 2 e^- \rightarrow Ca(s)$	−2.84
$Cu^{2+}(aq) + 2 e^- \rightarrow Cu(s)$	0.34	$Zn^{2+}(aq) + 2 e^- \rightarrow Zn(s)$	−0.76
$Fe^{3+}(aq) + e^- \rightarrow Fe^{2+}(aq)$	0.77	$Cd^{2+}(aq) + 2 e^- \rightarrow Cd(s)$	−0.40
$2 H^+(aq) + 2 e^- \rightarrow H_2(g)$	0.00	$Fe^{2+}(aq) + 2 e^- \rightarrow Fe(s)$	−0.44

$H_2O_2(aq) + 2 H^+(aq) + 2 e^- \rightarrow 2 H_2O(l)$	1.76
$O_2(g) + 4 H^+(aq) + 4 e^- \rightarrow 2 H_2O(l)$	1.23
$MnO_4^-(aq) + 8 H^+(aq) + 5 e^- \rightarrow Mn^{2+}(aq) + 4 H_2O(l)$	1.51
$Ag(S_2O_3)_2^{3-}(aq) + e^- \rightarrow Ag(s) + 2 S_2O_3^{2-}(aq)$	0.02
$Fe(CN)_6^{3-}(aq) + e^- \rightarrow Fe(CN)_6^{4-}$	0.36
$Fe(CN)_6^{4-} + 2 e^- \rightarrow Fe(s) + 6 CN^-(aq)$	−1.16

where both half-cell potentials refer to reductions as in Table 15-1. We got this result by first combining the $\Delta G°$ values and then computing $E°$. The half-cell potentials combine without adjusting for the stoichiometric coefficients because $E°$ is an *intensive* property of the half-cell reaction, independent of the amount. $\Delta G°$ is an *extensive* property and stoichiometric coefficients must be considered when computing $\Delta G°$.

Example 3. Compute the standard half-cell potential for

$$Fe^{3+}(aq) + 3\ e^- \rightarrow Fe(s)$$

From Table 15-1, we have

$$Fe^{3+}(aq) + e^- \rightarrow Fe^{2+}(aq) \qquad E_1° = +0.77\ V$$
$$Fe^{2+}(aq) + 2\ e^- \rightarrow Fe(s) \qquad E_2° = -0.44\ V$$

Adding the two half-cell reactions, we get the desired one, but this time we can't just add the $E°$'s. First convert to $\Delta G°$'s, and then add:

$$Fe^{3+}(aq) + e^- \rightarrow Fe^{2+}(aq) \qquad \Delta G_1° = -2FE_1°$$
$$Fe^{2+}(aq) + 2\ e^- \rightarrow Fe(s) \qquad \Delta G_2° = -FE_2°$$
$$Fe^{3+}(aq) + 3\ e^- \rightarrow Fe(s) \quad \Delta G_3° = \Delta G_1° + \Delta G_2°$$

$$\Delta G_3° = \Delta G_1° + \Delta G_2° = -2FE_1° - FE_2° = -3FE_3°$$
$$E_3° = (2E_1° + E_2°)/3 = +0.37\ V$$

Standard half-cell potentials can be used to compute free energy changes and equilibrium constants for many reactions other than oxidation-reduction reactions.

Example 4. Compute the formation constant for $Fe(CN)_4^{3-}$, i.e., K for

$$Fe^{2+}(aq) + 6\ CN^-(aq) \rightleftarrows Fe(CN)_6^{4-}(aq)$$

From Table 15-1, we find the half-cell potentials:

$$Fe^{2+}(aq) + 2\ e^- \rightarrow Fe(s) \qquad E° = -0.44\ V$$
$$Fe(CN)_6^{4-} + 2\ e^- \rightarrow Fe(s) + 6\ CN^-(aq) \qquad E° = -1.16\ V$$

Subtracting the two half-cell reactions gives the desired equilibrium. Thus $\Delta G° = -2F\ (-0.44) - (-2F)(-1.16) = -1.44\ F$ or $\Delta G° = -139\ kJ$, and $K = 2.3 \times 10^{24}$.

Concentration Cells and the Glass Electrode

Consider a galvanic cell with two Cu electrodes in contact with 0.100 and 0.00100 M solutions of $Cu(NO_3)_2$. The standard potential of the cell is $E° = 0.000\ V$. The half-cell and overall cell reactions are:

$$Cu^{2+}(aq,\ 0.1\ M) + 2\ e^- \rightarrow Cu(s)$$
$$Cu(s) \rightarrow Cu^{2+}(aq,\ 0.001\ M) + 2\ e^-$$

$$Cu^{2+}(aq, 0.1 \text{ M}) \rightarrow Cu^{2+}(aq, 0.001 \text{ M})$$

The Nernst equation predicts the cell potential:

$$E = 0.000 - \frac{0.0592}{2} \log \frac{0.001}{0.1} = 0.0592 \text{ V}$$

Such a cell is called a *concentration cell* since the potential depends only on the concentration ratio for two, otherwise identical, half-cells.

This result can be put to good use. Suppose that we want to determine the concentration of a Cu^{2+} solution. We could place a sample of the solution in contact with a Cu electrode, and join this half-cell with another Cu^{2+}/Cu half-cell with precisely known Cu^{2+} concentration. The potential of the resulting cell would be a measure of the unknown Cu^{2+} concentration. The Cu electrode in contact with the Cu^{2+} solution of unknown concentration is called an *indicator electrode*, since it "indicates" the unknown concentration.

An indicator electrode for [Cl⁻] can be constructed by coating a Ag electrode with insoluble AgCl. The half-cell reaction then is:

$$AgCl(s) + e^- \rightarrow Ag(s) + Cl^-(aq)$$

A cell consisting of two Ag/AgCl electrodes in contact with solutions of known and unknown [Cl⁻] will develop a potential:

$$E = 0.000 - \frac{0.0592}{1} \log \frac{[Cl^-]_{unknown}}{[Cl^-]_{known}}$$

The Ag/AgCl electrode is most commonly used as a *secondary reference electrode*. The hydrogen electrode, the primary reference electrode, is inconvenient to use in practice, since it requires $H_2(g)$ and a specially prepared Pt electrode at which the half-reaction is reversible. Thus secondary reference electrodes are usually used in practical electrochemical measurements. A common design for a Ag/AgCl electrode is shown in Figure 15-2. The electrode consists of a Ag wire coated with AgCl, and contained in a tube filled with 0.100 M KCl solution. The tube makes contact with the outer solution through a fiber which allows electrical contact, but with negligible flow of solution.

The Ag/AgCl electrode acts as a Cl⁻ indicator electrode because the current which flows to or from such an electrode is carried entirely by Cl⁻ ions. Thus the potential between two Ag/AgCl electrodes is related to the ratio of [Cl⁻] in contact with the two electrodes. In general, if the electric current is carried by a single species, the potential between solutions A and B is proportional to the logarithm of the concentration ratio C_A/C_B.

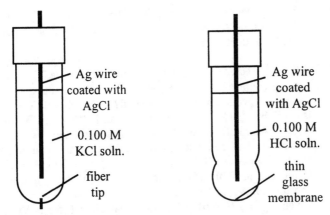

Figure 15-2. A Ag/AgCl electrode. **Figure 15-3.** A pH-sensitive glass electrode.

This result has an important application in electrochemical pH measurements (the pH meter) using a *glass electrode*. A thin membrane of glass can conduct a small electrical current and, in most circumstances, it behaves as though the current carrier is H^+. Thus the potential across a glass membrane is proportional to the logarithm of the concentration ratio $[H^+]_{inside}/[H^+]_{outside}$. The glass electrode is usually used with another Ag/AgCl/KCl electrode in contact with the test solution. Thus there are three potential-determining processes:

$$AgCl(s) + e^- \rightarrow Ag(s) + Cl^-(aq, 0.100\ M)$$
$$H^+(aq, 0.100\ M) \rightarrow H^+(aq, \text{test solution})$$
$$Cl^-(aq, 0.100\ M) + Ag(s) \rightarrow AgCl(s) + e^-$$

Since both Ag/AgCl electrodes are in contact with the same $[Cl^-]$, the potential is determined by the logarithm of the $[H^+]$ concentration ratio, and thus is related to the pH of the test solution:

$$E = 0.000 - 0.0592 \log\frac{[H^+]_{\text{test soln.}}}{0.100\ M} = 0.0592(\text{pH} - 1)$$

Problems

15.1 How many grams of (a) Ag, (b) Zn, and (c) Fe would be deposited by passing 0.200 mol of electrons from solutions of $AgNO_3$, $Zn(NO_3)_2$, and $Fe(NO_3)_3$? *Ans.* (a) 21.6, (b) 6.54, (c) 3.72 g

15.2 How long would it take to deposit 100 g Al from an electrolysis cell containing Al_2O_3 at a current of 125 A? Assume that Al is the only product formed at the cathode.

Ans. 2.48 hours

15.3 What is the standard potential of a cell that uses the Zn^{2+}/Zn and Ag^+/Ag couples? When the cell is allowed to produce an electric current, which metal is deposited? *Ans. 1.56 V, Ag*

15.4 Is (a) $FeBr_3$, (b) FeI_3 stable? That is, can Fe^{3+} oxidize Br^- or I^-?

Ans. $FeBr_3$ is stable, FeI_3 reacts to produce Fe^{2+} and I_2.

15.5 What is the half-cell potential for the MnO_4^-/Mn^{2+} couple when $[MnO_4^-] = [Mn^{2+}]$, $[H^+] = 10^{-4}$ M? *Ans. E = 1.04 V*

15.6 From data in Table 15-1, calculate the formation equilibrium constant for $Ag(S_2O_3)_2^{3-}$ at 25°C. *Ans. $K_f = 1.6 \times 10^{13}$*

15.7 Given $K_{sp} = 1.6 \times 10^{-10}$ for AgCl, calculate E for a Ag/AgCl electrode immersed in 0.100 M KCl at 25°C. *Ans. E = 0.28 V*

15.8 Calculate the potential of a cell consisting of two Ag/AgCl electrodes, one in contact with 0.100 M KCl, the other in contact with 1.0×10^{-5} M NaCl. *Ans. E = 0.237 V*

15.9 Calculate the potential of a cell consisting of a glass electrode filled with 0.100 M HCl, a Ag/AgCl electrode in contact with 0.100 M KCl, both immersed in a solution with pH = 4.35.

Ans. 0.198 V

15.10 What is the potential of a cell containing two H^+/H_2 electrodes, one in contact with 10^{-8} M H^+, the other in contact with 0.025 M H^+? *Ans. 0.379 V*

15.11 Use the half-cell, $HO_2^- + H_2O + 2\ e^- \rightarrow 3\ OH^-$, $E° = +0.88$ V, with other information in Table 15-1 to compute the pK_a of H_2O_2 at 25°C. *Ans. $pK_a = 12.2$*

15.12 If the standard Tl^{3+}/Tl^+ and Tl^+/Tl half-cell potentials are 1.25 and −0.34 V, what is $E°$ for Tl^{3+}/Tl? *Ans. $E° = 0.72$ V*

IN THIS CHAPTER:

✔ *Empirical Rate Laws*
✔ *Mechanisms of Reactions*

Introduction

A process is spontaneous if ΔG is negative, but knowing that a process is spontaneous doesn't mean that it will occur at a measurable rate. A piece of graphite in air is thermodynamically unstable—ΔG is large and negative for the conversion to CO_2, but the rate is negligible until we raise the temperature, at which point the carbon burns spontaneously.

In this chapter, we examine the rates of chemical reactions. The first section deals with empirical rate laws, equations that summarize experimental rate measurements. Rate laws can often be understood in terms of the mechanisms of the reactions, and the derivation of rate laws from a postulated mechanism is the subject of the second section.

Empirical Rate Laws

Reaction Rates. Consider a general reaction,
$$A + 3 B \rightarrow 2 C \qquad (16\text{-}1)$$

We describe the rate of the reaction in terms of the rate of disappearance of one of the reactants or the rate of appearance of the product,

$$\frac{\Delta[A]}{\Delta t}, \ \frac{\Delta[B]}{\Delta t}, \ \text{or} \ \frac{\Delta[C]}{\Delta t}$$

The stoichiometry of the reaction tells us that in time interval Δt, $\Delta[B] = 3 \ \Delta[A]$, $\Delta[C] = -2 \ \Delta[A]$; furthermore, $\Delta[A]$ and $\Delta[B]$ are negative, $\Delta[C]$ is positive. Thus we must include an appropriate sign and stoichiometric coefficient in expressing the rate of the reaction:

$$\text{Rate} = -\frac{\Delta[A]}{\Delta t} = -\frac{1}{3}\frac{\Delta[B]}{\Delta t} = \frac{1}{2}\frac{\Delta[C]}{\Delta t} \tag{16-2}$$

It is most common to express rates in terms of molar concentrations of species, even for gas-phase reactions. The usual units of a reaction rate are mol $L^{-1}s^{-1}$.

When a reaction is slow enough, it is appropriate to express the rate as the ratio of a concentration change, $\Delta[A]$, to a time interval, Δt, but when the reaction is faster, we consider the limit as Δt approaches zero, the first derivative of [A] with respect to time:

$$\text{Rate} = -\frac{d[A]}{dt} = -\lim_{\Delta t \to 0} \frac{\Delta[A]}{\Delta t} \tag{16-3}$$

Concentration Dependence. The rate of a reaction often depends on reactant concentrations, sometimes on product concentrations, and occasionally on the concentration of a species, X, which is not involved in the stoichiometric reaction. The dependence on concentrations can often be expressed by an equation, called the *empirical rate law*:

$$\text{Rate} = k \ [A]^a \ [B]^b \ [C]^c \ [X]^x \tag{16-4}$$

In Eq. (16-4), k is called the *rate constant*, the exponents a, b, c, and x are called *orders*. The orders are usually integers, but may be fractions such as 1/2 or 2/3. A positive order a means that the rate increases with [A], a negative order c means that the rate decreases with increasing [C]. If the rate depends on [X] and $x > 0$, we say that X is a *catalyst* which increases the rate; if $x < 0$, we say that X is an inhibitor which decreases the rate. The sum of all the individual orders is called the *overall order of the reaction*. Despite the apparent similarity of an empirical rate law to an equilibrium constant expression, the orders are not necessarily equal to stoichiometric coefficients.

Suppose in a reaction whose rate depends only on [A] and [B] that $a = 1$ and $b = 2$; the overall order then is 3. We say that the reaction rate is *first-order* in A, *second-order* in B, and *third-order* overall. The units of Rate are mol $L^{-1}s^{-1}$, and [A] [B]^2 has units $(mol/L)^3$, the rate constant k has units $(mol/L)^{-2}s^{-1}$. The units of k depend on the overall order of the reaction.

You Need to Know

Rate law for reaction, A + B → Products:
$$\text{Rate} = - d[A]/dt = -d[B]/dt = k[A]^a[B]^b[X]^x$$

- Rate has units $mol\ L^{-1}s^{-1}$
- a, b, x are orders in A, B, and X
- Overall order, $n = a + b + x$
- X is a catalyst if $x > 0$, an inhibitor if $x < 0$
- Units of rate constant k, $(mol/L)^{1-n}s^{-1}$.

Determination of Rate Laws. The simplest way to determine a rate law is the *method of initial rates*. If a reaction is slow enough, it can be allowed to proceed for a short time, Δt, and the change in a reactant or product concentration measured. Repeating the experiment for different concentrations, the concentration-dependence of the rate can be deduced.

Example 1. For the reaction, A + B → C, three rate experiments yielded the data shown in the first four columns of the table, where $[A]_0$ and $[A]_f$ are [A] values at the beginning and end of the experiment, repetively:

$[A]_0$/M	$[B]_0$/M	Δt/min	$[A]_f$/M	Init. Rate
0.1000	1.00	5.0	0.0975	5.0×10^{-4} M/min
0.1000	2.00	5.0	0.0900	2.0×10^{-3} M/min
0.0500	1.00	10.0	0.0475	2.5×10^{-4} M/min

Determine the orders of the reaction in A and B, the overall order, and the rate constant k.

Since we know $\Delta[A]$ for the three experiments, the initial rate is

$$\text{Rate} = - \Delta[A]/\Delta t$$

and these values are given in the fifth column of the table. Compare the first and second experiments. [A] was held constant, [B] was doubled, and the rate increased by a factor of 4; we conclude that the reaction is second-order in B. Compare the first and third experiments where [B] was constant and [A] was halved; the rate decreased by a factor of 2, and we conclude that the reaction is first-order in A. Thus the reaction is third-order overall. The first experiment gives:

$$\text{Rate} = k\,[A]\,[B]^2$$
$$5.0 \times 10^{-4} \text{ mol L}^{-1}\text{min}^{-1} = k\,(0.1000 \text{ mol/L})(1.00 \text{ mol/L})^2$$
$$k = 5.0 \times 10^{-3} \text{ (mol/L)}^{-2}\text{min}^{-1}$$

Analysis of Concentration vs. Time Data. Another way of determining a reaction order is to carry out a reaction with all reactants but one at high concentrations which change very little as the low-concentration reactant is consumed. The changing concentration is measured from time to time.

In effect, the rate depends only on the changing concentration since all others are nearly constant. Thus the rate can be expressed as:

$$\text{Rate} = k'\,[A]^a \tag{16-5}$$

where k', which includes the true rate constant k and all the other, nearly constant, concentrations, raised to the appropriate power, is called a *pseudo-a-order rate constant*. Using the methods of integral calculus, it can be shown that the time-dependence of [A] is:

$$a \neq 1 \qquad\qquad [A]^{1-a} = [A]_0^{1-a} + (a - 1)\,k't \tag{16-6}$$

$$a = 1 \qquad\qquad \ln [A] = \ln [A]_0 - k't \tag{16-7}$$

Thus a plot of $[A]^{1-a}$ or $\ln [A]$ vs. time should give a straight line. The plot resulting in a straight line determines the order in A, and the slope of the line is $(a - 1)\,k'$ or $-k'$.

Example 2. At a certain elevated temperature, the following reaction occurs:

$$CH_3CH_2Cl(g) \rightarrow CH_2CH_2(g) + HCl(g)$$

The following data were obtained in a rate experiment:

t/min	[CH_3CH_2Cl]	t/min	[CH_3CH_2Cl]	t/min	[CH_3CH_2Cl]
0	1.19×10^{-2}	10	5.8×10^{-3}	30	1.4×10^{-3}
5	8.3×10^{-3}	20	2.9×10^{-3}	50	0.3×10^{-3}

Determine the order of the reaction in CH_3CH_2Cl.

Plots of $\ln$ [CH_3CH_2Cl] and $1/$[CH_3CH_2Cl] vs t are shown in Figure 16-1. The log plot is clearly much more linear than the reciprocal plot. Thus we conclude that the reaction is first-order in CH_3CH_2Cl. The slope of the straight line gives the rate constant $k = 0.073$ min^{-1}. In this case, there is no other species at high concentration, so the rate law is:

$$\text{Rate} = (0.073\ \text{min}^{-1})\ [\text{CH}_3\text{CH}_2\text{Cl}]$$

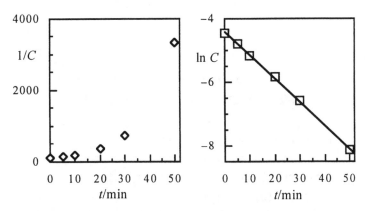

Figure 16-1. Second- and first-order plots for data of Example 2.

Determination of Rate Law:

1. Initial rate as function of concentration.
2. Limiting reagent concentration vs. time: first-order: ln [A] vs. *t* gives straight line, *n*-order: $[A]^{1-n}$ vs. *t* gives straight line ($n \neq 1$).

Temperature Dependence of Rate Constants. Rate constants, like equilibrium constants, are temperature-dependent. Unlike K, however, k virtually always increases with increasing temperature. The temperature-dependence usually obeys the *Arrhenius equation*,

$$k = A\, e^{-E_a/RT} \tag{16-8}$$

where A is called the *frequency factor* and E_a is the *activation energy*. The logarithmic form of the Arrhenius equation,

$$\ln k = \ln A - \frac{E_a}{RT}$$

has the same form as eq (12-14) for ln K, with E_a replacing $\Delta H°$ and ln A replacing $\Delta S°/R$. Comparing rate constants measured at two different temperatures, we can derive thte analog of Eq. (12-15):

$$\ln \frac{k_1}{k} = \frac{E_a}{R}\left(\frac{1}{T_2} - \frac{1}{T_1}\right)$$

(16–9)

Important Information

Arrhenius equation, $k = Ae^{-Ea/RT}$, gives the temperature dependence of a rate constant, A = frequency factor, E_a = activation energy.

Mechanisms of Reactions

A chemical equation accurately portrays the nature of the starting and final materials in a chemical reaction, but the arrow conveniently covers our ignorance of what happens in between. How many steps are there in the overall process? What are the spatial and energetic requirements in each step? What is the rate of each step? Although rate measurements usually describe only the overall reaction, the measurement of rates under different conditions often contribute to an understanding of the mechanism.

Elementary Reactions. A *reaction mechanism* consists of a series of *elementary reaction steps*, the sum of which is the stoichiometric chemical equation. An elementary reaction is a precise statement of the molecules which react or are formed in a single step of a mechanism. When we write a mechanism with its elementary reaction steps, we are forming a hypothesis that we hope to test with experimental rate data. The first step in such a test is to derive the rate law expected from the postulated mechanism.

The *molecularity* specifies the number of molecules involved as reactants in an elementary step. A *unimolecular* reaction is a step in which a single A molecule undergoes a reaction; the rate of such a step is first-order, $k_1[A]$. A *bimolecular* reaction is a step in which two molecules react, A + B or 2 A; the rate of such a step is first-order in each reacting species, $k_2[A][B]$ or $k_2[A]^2$. A *termolecular* reaction is a step in which three molecules react, A + B + C or 2 A + B or 3 A; the rate of such a step is first-order in each reacting species and third-order overall.

Energetics of a Reaction. Most molecular collisions do not result in reaction. Even if the requisite number of molecules come together, only those possessing enough energy, usually far in excess of the average energy, can undergo the violent distortions of bond lengths and angles necessary for the rearrangements that lead to chemical reaction. The activation energy, E_a, is a measure of the excess energy needed for molecules to react, and the exponential term in the Arrhenius equation approximates the fraction of molecules possessing this excess energy.

The *activated complex* is that combination of reacting molecules having the excess energy needed to rearrange to form products. For a reversible reaction, the same activated complex must be formed for both the forward and reverse reaction. Thus, for reactions carried out at constant pressure,

$$E_a(\text{forward}) - E_a(\text{reverse}) = \Delta H \qquad (16\text{-}10)$$

This relationship is shown graphically in Figure 16-2 where the energy of a reacting system is plotted vs. *reaction coordinate*, showing the increase in energy as reactants are converted to the activated complex and the decrease in energy as activated complex is converted to products.

In a mechanism involving several elementary steps, each involving an activated complex, the highest energy activated complex determines the *rate-limiting step* of the mechanism.

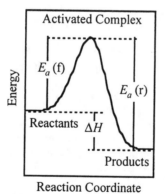

Figure 16-2. Energy vs. reaction coordinate for a reversible process.

Thus for the reaction of Example 1, the activated complex for the rate-limiting step has composition AB_2, and the rate-limiting step may be the

Essential Point

Reaction mechanism: A postulated series of elementary steps showing the transformation of reactants to products. A mechanism must be consistent with experiment as follows:

- Sum of elementary steps = balanced equation.
- Empirical rate law, if it has only integral positive powers of the species concentrations, may express the molecularity of the rate-limiting step.
- Empirical rate law derivable from mechanism.

termolecular approach of one molecule of A with two of B.

Example 3. The reactions,
$$CH_3CH_2Br + OH^- \rightarrow CH_3CH_2OH + Br^-$$
and
$$(CH_3)_3CBr + OH^- \rightarrow (CH_3)_3COH + Br^-$$
have rate laws: $Rate_1 = k_1 [CH_3CH_2Br][OH^-]$
and $Rate_2 = k_2 [(CH_3)_3CBr]$

The first reaction occurs in a single bimolecular elementary step in which OH^- displaces Br^- with the C-O bond forming as the C-Br bond is breaking. The $(CH_3)_3C$ group is too bulky to allow close approach of OH^-, so that in this case the rate-limiting step is unimolecular C-Br bond breaking, followed by a fast step in which the C-OH bond is formed:
$$(CH_3)_3CBr \rightarrow (CH_3)_3C^+ + Br^-$$
$$(CH_3)_3C^+ + OH^- \rightarrow (CH_3)_3COH$$

Example 4. The reaction in basic aqueous solution,
$$I^- + OCl^- \rightarrow OI^- + Cl^-$$
has the rate law: $Rate = k [I^-][OCl^-][OH^-]^{-1}$

Propose a mechanism and show that it is consistent with the observed rate law.

The appearence of a negative power of concentration, $[OH^-]$, introduces a new concept, the role of chemical equilibrium in regulating the concentrations of reactants or reaction intermediates. In this case, in Step 1 HOCl is formed in a straightforward reversible acid-base reaction.

Step 1: $\qquad\qquad OCl^- + H_2O \rightleftarrows HOCl + OH^-$

This reaction comes to equilibrium, at which the forward and reverse reactions occur at the same rate.

$$k_1 [OCl^-] = k_{-1} [HOCl][OH^-]$$

In this notation, k_1 is the rate constant for the forward reaction of Step 1 and k_{-1} is the rate constant for the reverse reaction.

From this, $\qquad\qquad [HOCl] = \dfrac{k_1 [OCl^-]}{k_{-1} [OH^-]}$

Step 2: HOCl then reacts with I^- in the rate-limiting irreversible step

$$HOCl + I^- \rightarrow HOI + Cl^-$$

$$rate = k_2 [HOCl][I^-]$$

Step 3: HOI reacts rapidly with OH^-.

$$HOI + OH^- \rightleftarrows OI^- + H_2O$$

The sum of the three steps corresponds to the stoichiometric equation, the rate of which is obtained from the equations of Steps 1 and 2.

$$Rate = \frac{k_1 k_2}{k_{-1}} \frac{[OCl^-][I^-]}{[OH^-]}$$

Problems

16.1 In an experiment involving the reaction, $N_2 + 3 H_2 \rightarrow 2 NH_3$, the rate was measured as $\Delta[NH_3]/\Delta t = 2.0 \times 10^{-4}$ mol $L^{-1}s^{-1}$. What is the rate expressed in terms of (a) $-\Delta[N_2]/\Delta t$ and (b) $-\Delta[H_2]/\Delta t$? *Ans.* (a) 1.0×10^{-4} M s, (b) 3.0×10^{-4} M s^{-1}

16.2 The reaction, $H_2(g) + Br_2(g) \rightarrow 2 HBr(g)$ has a rate given by the rate law, Rate $= k [H_2][Br_2]^{1/2}$. (a) What are the units of the rate constant k? (b) If the volume of the gas mixture is halved, by what factor is the rate changed?

Ans. (a) $(mol/L)^{-1/2}s^{-1}$, (b) 2.8

16.3 If the steady-state concentration of O_3 in a polluted atmosphere is 2.0×10^{-8} mol/L, the rate of production of O_3 is 7.2×10^{-13} M/hr, and O_3 is destroyed by the reaction, $2\,O_3 \rightarrow 3\,O_2$, what is the rate constant for the reaction, assuming a rate law, Rate $= -(1/2)\,\Delta[O_3]/\Delta t = k\,[O_3]^2$? *Ans.* 0.25 M^{-1}s^{-1}

16.4 In the enzymatic fermentation of sugar, the sugar concentration decreased from 0.12 M to 0.06 M in 10 hours, and to 0.03 M in 20 hours. What is the order of the reaction? What is the rate constant k? *Ans.* (a) first-order, (b) 6.9×10^{-2} hr^{-1}

16.5 The rate law for the reaction, $Ce^{4+}(aq) + Fe^{2+}(aq) \rightarrow Ce^{3+}(aq) + Fe^{3+}(aq)$, is: Rate $= (1.0 \times 10^3$ M^{-1}s$^{-1})\,[Ce^{4+}][Fe^{2+}]$. If 0.500 L of 0.0020 M $Ce(SO_4)_2$ is rapidly mixed with 0.500 L of 0.0020 M $FeSO_4$, how long does it take for $[Fe^{2+}]$ to decrease to 1.0×10^{-4} M? *Ans.* 9.0 s

16.6 The reaction, $CH_3Cl(aq) + H_2O(l) \rightarrow CH_3OH(aq) + H^+(aq) + Cl^-(aq)$, is first-order in CH_3Cl with $k = 3.32 \times 10^{-10}$ s^{-1} at 25°C and 3.13×10^{-9} s^{-1} at 40°C. What is the activation energy? *Ans.* 116 kJ/mol

16.7 The *trans* $\rightarrow$ *cis* isomerization of 1,2-dichloroethylene proceeds with $E_a = 231$ kJ/mol and $\Delta H = 4.2$ kJ/mol. What is E_a for the *cis* $\rightarrow$ *trans* isomerization? *Ans.* 227 kJ/mol

16.8 The reaction, $2\,A + 2\,B \rightarrow C + D$, gave initial rate data as shown in the table below. Determine the rate law and evaluate the rate constant.

[A]/M	[B]/M	Rate/M s^{-1}
2.0×10^{-3}	2.0×10^{-4}	1.5×10^{-6}
4.0×10^{-3}	2.0×10^{-4}	6.0×10^{-6}
4.0×10^{-3}	6.0×10^{-4}	1.8×10^{-5}

Ans. Rate $= (1.9 \times 10^3$ M^{-2}s$^{-1})\,[A]^2[B]$

16.9 The reaction, $2\,NO(g) + O_2(g) \rightarrow 2\,NO_2(g)$, proceeds according to the rate law, Rate $= k\,[NO][O_2]$. Propose a mechanism consistent with this rate law.

Ans. (i) $NO + O_2 \rightarrow ONOO$ (slow)
(ii) $ONOO + NO \rightarrow 2\,NO_2$ (fast)

Appendix

Table of Atomic Masses
(Atomic Numbers 1-92)

Name	A	Mass	Name	A	Mass
Actinium, Ac	89	227.028	Hafnium, Hf	72	178.49
Aluminum, Al	13	26.9815	Helium, He	2	4.00260
Antimony, Sb	51	121.757	Holmium, Ho	67	164.930
Argon, A	18	39.948	Hydrogen, H	1	1.00794
Arsenic, As	33	74.922	Indium, In	49	114.82
Astatine, At	85	(210)	Iodine, I	53	126.904
Barium, Ba		137.33	Iridium, Ir	77	192.22
Beryllium, Be	4	9.01218	Iron, Fe	26	55.847
Bismuth, Bi	83	208.980	Krypton, Kr	36	83.80
Boron, B	5	10.81	Lanthanum, La	57	138.906
Bromine, Br	35	v79.904	Lead, Pb	82	207.2
Cadmium, Cd	48	112.41	Lithium, Li	3	6.941
Calcium, Ca	20	40.078	Lutetium, Lu	71	174.967
Carbon, C	6	12.011	Magnesium, Mg	12	24.305
Cerium, Ce	58	v140.12	Manganese, Mn	25	54.9380
Cesium, Cs	55	132.905	Mercury, Hg	80	200.59
Chlorine, Cl	17	35.453	Molybdenum, Mo	42	95.94
Chromium, Cr	24	51.996	Neodymium, Nd	60	144.24
Cobalt, Co	27	58.9332	Neon, Ne	10	20.1797
Copper, Cu	29	63.546	Nickel, Ni	28	58.69
Dysprosium, Dy	66	162.50	Niobium, Nb	41	92.9064
Erbium, Er	68	167.26	Nitrogen, N	7	14.0067
Europium, Eu	63	151.96	Osmium, Os	76	190.2
Fluorine, F	9	18.9984	Oxygen, O	8	15.9994
Francium, Fr	87	(223)	Palladium, Pd	46	106.42
Gadolinium, Gd	64	157.25	Phosphorus, P	15	30.9738
Gallium, Ga	31	69.72	Platinum, Pt	78	195.08
Germanium, Ge	32	72.61	Polonium, Po	84	(209)
Gold, Au	79	196.967	Potassium, K	19	39.0983

Praseodymium, Pr	59	140.908	Tantalum, Ta	73	180.948
Promethium, Pm	61	(145)	Technetium, Tc	43	(98)
Protactinium, Pa	91	231.036	Tellurium, Te	52	127.60
Radium, Ra	99	226.024	Terbium, Tb	65	158.925
Radon, Rn	86	(222)	Thallium, Tl	81	204.383
Rhenium, Re	75	186.207	Thorium, Th	90	232.038
Rhodium, Rh	45	102.906	Thulium, Tm	69	168.934
Rubidium, Rb	37	85.4678	Tin, Sn	50	118.710
Ruthenium, Ru	44	101.07	Titanium, Ti	22	47.88
Samarium, Sm	62	150.36	Tungsten, W	74	183.84
Scandium, Sc	21	44.9559	Uranium, U	92	238.029
Selenium, Se	34	78.96	Vanadium, V	23	50.9415
Silicon, Si	14	28.0855	Xenon, Xe	54	131.29
Silver, Ag	47	107.868	Yttrium, Y	39	88.9058
Sodium, Na	11	22.9898	Zinc, Zn	30	65.39
Sulfur, S	16	32.066	Zirconium, Zr	40	91.224

A value in parentheses for an element without any stable nuclides is the atomic mass number of the isotope of that element with the longest known half-life.

Index

155